The MicroKidz

The time: the very near future.

The characters: Thor Benson, a fifteen-year-old computer whizz-kid
Kevin and Pamela Powell, his neighbours and friends.

They comprise the MicroKidz and, together with their high-tech computer know-how and Mr Chips, Thor's ingenious robot, they're heading for mystery and adventure.

Data Snatchers is the fourth MicroKidz Mystery.

**Also by the same author,
and available in Knight Books:**

The Cagey Bee Byte
Computer Mind Games
Fission Chips

THE MICROKIDZ MYSTERY ADVENTURES

Data Snatchers

G. P. JORDAN

KNIGHT BOOKS
Hodder and Stoughton

Copyright © 1984 by G. P. Jordan
First published in Canada by General Paperbacks 1984
First published in Great Britain by Knight Books 1985

British Library C.I.P.

Jordan, G. P.
 Data snatchers.—(The MicroKidz mystery adventures)
 I. Title II. Series
 813'.54[J]   PZ7

ISBN 0-340-37182-X

*The characters and situations in this book are entirely
imaginary and bear no relation to any real person or
actual happening*

This book is sold subject to the condition that it shall
not, by way of trade or otherwise, be lent, re-sold,
hired out or otherwise circulated without the
publisher's prior consent in any form of binding or
cover other than that in which it is published and
without a similar condition including this condition
being imposed on the subsequent purchaser.

Printed and bound in Great Britain for Hodder and
Stoughton Paperbacks, a division of Hodder and
Stoughton Ltd., Mill Road, Dunton Green, Sevenoaks,
Kent (Editorial Office: 47 Bedford Square, London,
WC1 3DP) by Richard Clay (The Chaucer Press) Ltd.,
Bungay, Suffolk

CHAPTER 1
Plane Trouble

"Who's going to win?"
"The best man!"
"The best woman!"
"The best person for the job!"
"And who is that?"
"The one with the most votes!"

Sooner or later, every conversation in the town of Stanton raised the election issue. The campaign to elect a mayor and a town council was in its final stage. Voting day was drawing near and a close race was forecast. In the spirit of democracy, many ordinary citizens had volunteered to help their chosen candidate.

The MicroKidz were no exception. Sixteen-year-old Kevin Powell was working on the campaign for Art Crandles. The reelection of Mayor Gwen Griffin involved all the efforts of his younger sister, Pamela.

Only Thor Benson felt left out. Though he was busy with the election, he was not working for either candidate. This was not his choice; it was the law. The fifteen-year-old computer expert had a part-time job at BenDaCon, his father's data consultants firm. Regulations forbade any of the staff from becoming involved in the campaigning because BenDaCon was in charge of supervising Stanton's —and the country's—first electronic voting day.

"How does it feel to be neutral?" Kevin had asked Thor one day.

"Like Switzerland," Thor told him. "Surrounded by all points of view, but staying out of everything."

Kevin and Pam understood his difficult position. His lifelong neighbors and best friends were devoting all their time and energy to campaign work. They were at the center of all the excitement, having fun, learning new things, and meeting interesting people. Thor couldn't get involved; he had to settle for just hearing about their daily adventures. He tried to console himself by reminding the Powells of the price they'd have to pay after it was all over.

"In a few days we'll be back to normal," he told Pam and Kevin. "This is only an election. Somebody has to win and somebody has to lose."

"At least I'm on the right side," Kevin said smugly.

"That's what you think!" challenged Pam.

"Save it for your canvassing! When you both get going, I feel like a referee."

Kevin and Pamela were glaring at each other. Tension between the pair was becoming intolerable. Their involvement in the election process had resulted in an intense sibling rivalry, as they sought to prove themselves through their work.

"I think we need a break from all this," Thor continued. "No talk about politics or your work. Okay?"

"Then tell us about yours."

Thor grinned at the girl. When Pamela wanted to know what he was working on, she wanted to know everything. Thor didn't mind. She was a very special person to him. He hesitated calling her his girlfriend, even though she was the only girl he counted as a best friend. They were both shy persons, comfortable with each other, who sensed that time was on their side.

"Need a break, huh?" Kevin considered. "Let's wheel out of town."

He hurried out to switch on the electric fueler of his sports car.

Thor and Pam followed at a slower pace. Thor felt more at ease, now that the election arguments had stopped. The quarreling really disturbed him. He and the Powells had grown up together and he felt as close to them as a brother. Since Thor was an only child, the relationship was extra special to him.

On another level, the trio had a more celebrated alliance. The national press called them "The MicroKidz" because of their ingenuity with microtechnology. In a recent adventure, the three youngsters had discovered that hazardous material was being pirated from an obsolete nuclear generating station. This radioactive waste, *FISSION CHIPS*, posed a terrible threat to the population. Only by putting themselves at risk were the MicroKidz able to solve the mystery and avert a major tragedy.

"Drive safely, Kevin."

"Pammy, safety is my middle name."

"Not the last time I checked."

"If you don't like it, walk!"

"Drop it!" demanded Thor.

They apologized, but the tension remained close to the surface.

"Am I ever going to be thankful next week," Thor thought silently. "I can't stand this constant arguing. Too bad there isn't any way they can both win."

The sports car pulled out onto Matrix Boulevard and was soon speeding along the Cartesian Freeway. Traffic was light, and the convertible top was off; perfect conditions for a leisurely drive. Pam was squeezed comfortably into the rear seat behind her brother. She watched Thor adjust the compact disc sound system. Music filled their ears and the world seemed to revolve around Stanton.

"Where are we going?" Pam shouted above the music.

Thor shrugged. Anywhere was fine with him.

Kevin replied, "A surprise visit."

"What's the surprise?"

"They don't know we're coming!"

At the end of the freeway, they drove onto the old Farmline Road. The surrounding pasture land was dotted with herds of sheep and cattle. Agriculture had been the only business in Stanton prior to the high-tech industry that sprouted here ten years ago. Companies needed open space for warehouses and a break from big city stress. Many technicians took an interest in the area, adapted their experimental sciences, and as a result increased crop and livestock yields. This was an unexpected byproduct of the microchip success story.

"So who is this person we're going to see?"

"Just wait, Pam. You'll see."

"Come on, tell her, Kev. I'm wondering, too."

Kevin turned the volume low as they cornered onto a paved driveway. Ahead of them was a luxurious mansion shrouded behind willow trees. Thor recognized the building from a recent Satellite News Network report.

"I don't think this is such a great idea," he muttered.

Kevin ignored his words and continued up the drive.

Two vans were parked in front of the country mansion. Election signs had been plastered onto the sides of the vans, declaring: "FOR MAYOR, IT'S ART CRANDLES."

Pamela sunk low into her seat. This surprise visit into

enemy territory was not appreciated. Art Crandles was fighting a bitter campaign against the reelection of Mayor Gwen Griffin.

"Thanks for nothing, Kevin. Didn't Thor ask us to take a break from all this?"

Kevin replied by slamming the car door. Pam and Thor watched him approach the mansion entrance. After identifying himself on the video intercom, Kevin entered.

"Why would he do this?"

"To get on your nerves."

"Doesn't it bother you?"

Thor shrugged. "Yeah. But what can I do? He's taking his election work to heart."

"So am I! But Kevin's turned it into a personal battle."

Again Thor tried to restore calm. He was hurt by the growing division between brother and sister. After suggesting they relax from campaign pressures, it puzzled him that Kevin would come to this place.

"Maybe he intends to recruit us."

"Not a chance," winced Pamela. "There's something about Crandles I don't like. Beyond his policies. He comes in here out of the blue and claims to be the perfect choice. But what has he done?"

"Bought a nice home," Thor pointed out with a chuckle. "You're right, though. The way he's campaigning, you'd think he was running for the Presidency, not mayor of Stanton."

The mansion door opened and Kevin returned. He was carrying a package of floppy diskettes.

"What's that?"

"Top secret."

"Kevin, don't be smart."

"Sorry, Pammy. You're the opposition."

The sports car swung around the circular driveway. When they reached the end, Kevin turned to his offended passengers.

"Listen, I had no intention of coming here when we left town. We just happened to be in the area." Holding the diskettes, he added, "And I had to pick these up sometime."

He jerked the steering wheel and accelerated, turning the music up as they sped along Farmline Road. It seemed Kevin was trying to leave their disagreements behind.

Passing over these country hills, Thor recalled the last time he had traveled this route. He was with Pamela, returning to a summer computer camp. That adventure had brought them acclaim, and life since then had not been the same.

The music played on, the boys chatted, and Pamela finally began to relax. Gazing through the open convertible top, she watched cloud formations become imaginary objects. After awhile, her attention was distracted.

"Is there an airport nearby?" she wondered aloud.

"The Stanton Regional," Thor replied. "It's on the other side of town."

"Why are you asking?" Kevin joked. "Going someplace?"

"That plane over there," she said, pointing to a distant hill on the right. "Circling over those fields. Looks like it's getting ready to land."

"Probably on a private airstrip," Thor suggested. "A lot of these farmers have their own crop-dusters."

"But that doesn't look like a farm plane," she countered. "Reminds me of one of those small corporate jets. The kind your Dad travels on."

Thor observed the aircraft circling above the horizon. Kevin continued to drive along, ignoring the conversation.

He was more interested in listening to his compact disc player.

Pamela continued following the plane's flight pattern. It descended slowly and vanished from sight. Suddenly it climbed back into the sky. The pilot's actions were worrying her. Again the plane dipped toward the horizon. This time a tailspin accompanied the dive.

"Kevin! Pull over!"

Kevin was still singing along to the music and didn't hear her.

Thor was watching though and a feeling of dread overcame him too. The flight of that aircraft was dangerously faulty!

"Hey, what are you doing!" protested Kevin as Thor shut off the music player. Thor grappled for the dashboard cellular radio, pulled a panel off and dialed into the network.

"What's the aviation frequency?" he demanded.

Kevin passed on the numbers as he pulled the car to the side of the road. Thor punched in the code.

"...and power intermittent. Request landing coordinates," crackled the pilot's voice through their cellular radio speaker.

"An emergency!" exclaimed Kevin, for the first time seeing the distant aerial activity.

"I've been trying to tell you that!" Pam shivered.

"...forced landing! Open runway!" shouted the frantic voice.

Squawks and bleeps cut through their receiver. The signal became weaker as the airplane circled lower over the hills beyond.

"...can't read you, Echo One! Reserve power is negative! Come get us! Case secure! Repeat, case secure! We're going in!"

The youngsters listened helplessly to the desperate broadcast. They stood frozen in fear beside the car, watching another tailspin occur. This time, the aircraft disappeared.

A fireball erupted and clouds of black smoke rose up. Seconds later, they felt the shock wave of the explosion!

CHAPTER 2
An Impossible Rescue

"Emergency! Calling Stanton Regional Airport!"

Thor Benson gripped the microphone in his sweaty hands. An air traffic controller responded to his message. He checked the location and told the youth an emergency helicopter crew was being dispatched.

The burst of another fireball lit up the sky.

"I hope he bailed out in time," Pamela said.

"Anybody see a parachute?"

Kevin's question received no response. Uneasy that nothing was being done, he ran around and climbed into the driver's seat.

"Let's get over there! If the pilot made it, he'll need help fast!"

The MicroKidz were soon speeding toward the site. Two concession roads led to dead ends, resulting in more lost time. By their estimate, six minutes had elapsed since the explosions.

"There's the rescue copter!" Thor shouted.

They watched a blue jet helicopter race over the countryside. It proceeded in a direct route to the area. The black clouds of smoke swirled away as the jet copter landed.

"How close are we?" Pamela asked anxiously.

"Depends if this road goes through," Kevin answered.

Disappointment followed again. They came to another field fence. Two hills and a narrow valley separated the trio from the crash site. As Kevin reversed the car, Pam hit his shoulder.

"Look! It's leaving."

The blue jet copter climbed slowly into the sky. It hovered for a moment above the accident area before flying away.

"That should take care of it," murmured Kevin.

The consensus was that the survivors, if any, had been rescued. Further explosions caused by the aviation fuel or equipment on board might occur. It was best for the youngsters not to get too close to the wreckage of the aircraft.

"I want to go home," Thor said quietly.

His request was honored. The upsetting event had shaken them up. What had started as a simple drive into the country had ended with their witnessing a distant tragedy. Now they cared only for a quick return home.

"That another rescue crew?" Pam wondered aloud.

A red and white jet helicopter was flying overhead. Its colors and markings were familiar to them from a previous visit to the Stanton Regional Airport.

"Probably a backup unit," suggested Kevin. "They really seem to have it taken care of."

From the rear seat, Pamela viewed the descent. She saw the red and white copter circle as it landed amidst the faint smoke.

"At least we did something," she consoled herself. "Maybe our radio call saved a life. The most important thing is we tried."

Her attitude was shared by the trio. Along with their fascination for the high-tech world and computers, they shared a common desire to help others. When lives were in danger, they acted without hesitation.

"Can you drop me off in town?" asked Thor.
"Where?"
"Dad's office. Think I'll go in after all."
As the car neared the entrance ramp for the Cartesian Freeway, an electronic billboard lit up. A lightbeam was triggered by their approaching vehicle. "ART CRANDLES—FOR TOMORROW'S MAYOR," declared the lighting display. It featured a computer graphics portrait that made the smiling man's hands appear to wave.

"He may as well be waving bye-byes," scoffed Pam.
Thor looked around at the girl. His expression told her to keep silent. Kevin drove on, pretending to disregard her comment.

"How late will you be working?"
"That depends on how much has come in today," Thor replied to Kevin. "All the staff has been programming the electronic vote register for the last month. Some other clients are feeling neglected. So my Dad asked me to keep a check on those systems. Routine stuff."

"If you aren't programming the ballot, why can't you work on the mayor's campaign?" Pam wondered.

Thor shrugged. "Government orders. Nobody with access to the mainframe computer can be involved in any way. Just to be fair."

The Powells nodded in understanding. It was one of the few times they had agreed recently.

"What about these other clients? What sort of systems are you checking?"
"Come on, Pam. You know that's confidential."
"Nothing specific."

"You really are scanning," Thor chuckled. His friend's lively curiosity had been stirred. "Not to mention any names, but there is a store whose At-Home Shopping service is bonkers."

"Then how do the customers order?" wondered Kevin.

"The same way. But the store receives only their input dial code. They have to call back with an excuse like 'Just wanted to check that order.'"

"So why don't they just walk in to the store?" Kevin asked. Video home shopping was not his favorite topic.

"Do you go into a bank building for something that could be handled from your home system?"

Of course Kevin didn't, and Thor knew that. But he wanted to make the point that people were dependent on their At-Home Shopping and Banking services. The chance to compare different products over this fibre-optic relay system saved travel, time, effort, and money. Business was secure, service more efficient, and cash rarely changed hands. Electronic financial transfers were the standard.

"This system has made voting at home possible," continued Thor. "People can't use bad weather as an excuse for not casting a ballot. Choose your groceries, clothing, gifts—even a President—at the touch of a button."

The future had arrived in Stanton.

"How about letting me off at City Hall?" Pam requested.

She wanted to go the mayor's reelection headquarters but preferred not to say so directly. Thor realized that their day trying to disregard politics was history. His thoughts returned to the crash.

"I wonder what the news is on that plane?"

The others were trying to forget.

"I guess we'll hear later," he said, getting no reply.

They drove through the early afternoon traffic accompanied by music and headed into the center of Stanton. Cruising down Binary Avenue was a ritual, since it was the main street. It featured a broad sidewalk and was the town's prime people-watching zone.

"What a couple!" whistled Kevin.

A man and woman dressed in kimono-style clothing strolled past. The costumes were unusual, but what really drew attention to them was a fibre-optic display dangling between the couple. It changed colors and words, with one recurring message: "VOTE ART CRANDLES."

"The best yet!" stated Kevin.

"Oh yeah? Wait till you see what's planned for the mayor!"

"Won't do her any good."

The argument was about to resume. Fortunately, City Hall came into view. With its water sprinklers cooling the lawns surrounding the steel and glass building, it was an oasis in the center of the microchip boom town. Kevin drew over to park.

"I'll phone Mom and get a lift back," Pam told her brother. "Thanks."

"Bye, Pam," said Thor. "See you tonight."

"If I'm finished by then. There's a candidates' meeting."

Kevin remembered he also would be at that event. He wasn't looking forward to another confrontation with Pam.

"To BenDaCon?" he asked, referring to the Benson Data Consultants office.

Thor shrugged. "Cancel that. I can finish a couple of things in the workshop."

The boys cruised along Binary Avenue, enjoying the easygoing pace and friendly attitudes of the strollers. They spotted a few friends from their classes at Stanton High School, and Kevin beeped the horn at them. They waved back.

"What are you planning later?"

"Nothing really, why?"

"You said to Pam you'd see her. I just wondered if you two had something going."

"Not really. But if you want, call Cheryl and see what she's up to. Maybe we'll go out together."

Since Cheryl Tasel and Kevin had met a short while ago, they had spent many hours together. A classmate of Pamela's, Cheryl had become a pleasant addition to their circle of friends. She was out of town this week though, visiting relatives.

"So I have no excuse for not getting this done," Kevin said, touching the floppy diskette package.

"What's on them?"

"A Crandles victory plan."

"Too much! When can I see it?"

"Sorry, Thor. I promised."

"Hey, you can trust me."

"That's not the point. Anything to do with the election campaign is off-limits for you. Right?"

Kevin was right. Thor was an outsider to his closest friends.

"I can't wait for voting day," he said quietly. "The tension level in the whole town should drop by eighty degrees afterwards."

Kevin didn't respond. He was thinking ahead to the candidates' debate that night. They didn't speak again on the drive home. The only sound in the car was the music pumping from the car speakers.

"Drop over later," said Thor as they stopped in the Powells' driveway. "Maybe you'll need a second opinion on your diskettes."

"First I have to check on the data," Kevin said. "No offense, eh."

As he walked across the street to his home, Thor Benson

wondered even more at the extent politics motivated people. The thought of leaving town until after the election seemed attractive.

Above the front door of his house, a tiny blue light blinked to signal that the domestic security system was operating. Thor flipped open a digital switch and punched in the release code to prevent a false alarm from triggering.

"And where's Mr. Chips?" he wondered aloud.

The little robot came rumbling through the room as if he'd heard Thor asking for him. Assembled by Thor and Mr. Benson from a collection of spare parts, other robotic units, and a programmable micromemory, Mr. Chips was part of the family, the Bensons' house pet. The robot kept their house secure and had assisted in many MicroKidz adventures. Thor's mother said Mr. Chips earned his keep very well.

Thor heated a snack in the microwave oven and drank a glass of orange juice. He checked the electronic TeleMail service for messages and then walked out the back door to his lab.

He coded the digital deadbolt lock and entered his workshop lab behind the garage. Inside lay the jewels of his craft. Racks of salvaged electronics gear and tidbits of microtechnology crammed the room. Many inventions had been developed here, most of them yet to be patented.

Thor's pride and joy sat on the workbench desk. It was a modified CREX+ computer, recently rescued and restored from a bankrupt corporation. He had linked this high density computer to a bank of disk drives, external modems, a PIRX printer, and two display monitors. The memory capacity and computing power of this CREX+ surpassed newer models costing a hundred times more.

"I wonder if Dad is still talking to me?" he asked himself as he typed his private entry code to the BenDaCon offices onto the keyboard. Over miles of fibre-optic lines, Thor connected to his father's mainframe office computer. His LOG-ON response flashed positive.

"AC AS D." Thor typed the short from for "Access Assigned Data."

The video display monitor above the CREX+ lit up with a series of choices. He scanned the menu and selected one entry.

Data under "STANTON GIFT BOUTIQUE" appeared on the screen. This was the store undergoing the problems he had related to Pam and Kevin. Although customers were able to view the sales items on their home video systems, the purchase orders were not registering properly. BenDaCon had been contracted to solve the problem.

Thor ran his program tests. Everything returned in order. He tried a secret entry routine and still found the system intact. Yet, somehow, the security net was failing to hold requests for purchases. Why?

"Maybe I'll have to buy something to find out," he chuckled to himself.

He ordered the boutique's video catalogue onto the display. Hundreds of gift items were available. Thor decided to order at random.

"GLASSWARE—CRYSTAL," was chosen and he entered the appropriate numbers.

Choices continued to appear on the system's finely colored graphics. At-Home Shopping through fibre-optics had brought a new approach to merchandising. All the items seemed exceptionally appealing. He decided on a Waterford vase. Using the product number, he coded the micro, and to continue his test he ordered the gift to be delivered to Pamela Powell.

"THANK YOU FOR HOME SHOPPING THE STANTON GIFT

BOUTIQUE, PAMELA POWELL," displayed the monitor. "PLEASE ENTER YOUR BANKING CODE."

Thor paused. "Hmmm. Why not check if this is the breakpoint?"

From a separate data file, Thor picked out a financial transaction code. It was from the Election Office at City Hall, the department that had hired BenDaCon to regulate the voting.

"Now to find out who answers," he thought. "Maybe then I'll see where all this data is going."

While Thor was reaching for a stack of nearby floppy disks waiting to be sorted, a cursor dot appeared on the monitor. Thor was not watching as it zipped from right to left and swiped all his input data.

"You in there?" Kevin called from behind the door.

"It's open."

"Just didn't want to walk in on your top-secret work," Kevin drawled as he entered the workshop. He pulled up a swivel chair and leaned forward. "Are you willing to become an official witness?"

Thor knew instantly that Kevin could be referring to only one matter: the airplane accident.

"Call up the CompuNews line," he suggested.

Thor hit the code for that system to be delivered. The item popped onto the screen, and at the end the boys noted the special request.

"AN EMERGENCY CALL WAS RECEIVED FOLLOWING THE INCIDENT. AUTHORITIES WISH TO CONTACT THAT WITNESS...."

"Remember the blue helicopter?" asked Kevin, as the CompuNews line moved on to other stories.

"Sure, the rescue copter."

"No, it wasn't. The real rescue crew was on the second copter, the red and white one."

"How do you know that?"

"They said it in the earlier part of the report," Kevin said. Then he added slowly, "And wanna know something weird? There was no accident!"

"What? We saw it crash! And the flames! We heard the explosion!"

Kevin shook his head. "That wasn't from the plane."

CHAPTER 3
Finding the Time Code

"Come get us! Case secure! Repeat, case secure! We're going in!"

The tape recording stopped. Each word hung like a dark cloud in the conference room. Three men sat staring at Thor Benson and Kevin Powell.

"Yes, that's exactly what we heard," Thor stated.

"Then the plane went out of control and disappeared behind the hills," added Kevin.

The aviation investigators nodded. They asked how far the youths estimated they were from the crash and whether there were other aircraft in the vicinity.

"Only the blue helicopter," repeated Kevin.

One of the investigators, a chubby man named Hines, wanted more details. "Did you notice anything dangling from that copter? Possibly a cargo net?"

The boys shook their heads. "No sir. When it flew back into the sky after maybe two minutes on the ground, there was nothing hanging from it."

"If there was a cargo container, it was loaded inside," Thor suggested.

The three investigators conferred among themselves.

After a few moments, Hines turned to the boys. "That's all for now, fellows. Thanks for your cooperation."

As Hines escorted them to the hall elevator, Thor and Kevin raised questions of their own.

"What really happened out there, sir?"

"There was no crash, no bodies, nothing?" Kevin asked.

"That's correct," Hines told them. "Our control tower recorded those distress signals, but the plane had no flight plan or landing clearance. We reacted to the emergency and sent a rescue copter to the scene. And what did we find? An abandoned plane and a barn on fire!"

"What caused those explosions?"

"Propane tanks a farmer stored there," Hines muttered. "We still don't know how they ignited."

The elevator arrived. The boys had one last request.

"When you get any leads, would you please give us a call?"

A smile creased the man's face. He knew the MicroKidz by reputation from past adventures.

"*If* we do," the aviation investigator promised.

Kevin and Thor left the federal building with a new mystery to think about. Since they had responded to the request for witnesses and had related their experience to the government officials, both youths felt a strong connection to the case. Whatever had occurred on that abandoned airstrip now involved them.

"What's your next move?"

"To finish off that work for my Dad."

"Want a lift home?"

"No, thanks. It's only a few blocks to his office. May as well put in an appearance there. I have more chance of seeing him in his office than at the dinner table."

The two boys spoke about Mr. Benson's long working hours and agreed not to tell him anything about the air incident. He had enough on his mind straightening out the election ballot programming, without worrying about another mystery his son was probing.

They joined the sidewalk strollers along Binary Avenue. It seemed as if every fourth pedestrian wore a button stating his choice for mayor. Thor saw there was no place they could go to avoid the upcoming election. Inevitably their own conversation returned to it.

"Either way, someone new deserves a chance." Kevin picked up on one of his campaigning slogans. "I mean, Gwen Griffin has done a fair job for the past few years. But we need new blood. This town is bigger now, it's really a small city and needs to be governed like one."

"Keep talking, Kevin."

"What do you mean?"

"You need the practice. If you can't even change your sister's mind, then you'll really have to work on me!"

"Oh, come off it. The only reason Pam is supporting Gwen Griffin is because she's a woman."

The comment was hardly original. "And why are you helping Crandles? Because he's not?"

"This isn't a campaign of chromosomes."

"Then let the issues decide who to choose," said Thor. "And before you start comparing policies, save your breath. I'm impartial."

Reluctantly, Kevin dropped the subject. Walking alongside his friend, he thought ahead to that evening. He still had organization plans to finalize. As chairman of the Youth for Crandles committee, he had important duties.

"How late will you be working?"

"Depends on how much gets finished."

"Will you make it to the candidates' meeting?"

"Maybe. For entertainment only."

They understood each other's thoughts and feelings.

Political opinions would not upset their friendship. They could hold independent ideas, argue about them, and make up their own minds about the future.

Meanwhile, some things would always be the same.

"Wow! Here come my favorite ones yet!" Kevin whispered. Two girls, about eighteen years of age, were crossing the avenue. Wrapped around their necks were strands of fibre-optic filament, indiscreetly flashing "ART... ART...ART..."

Kevin could not resist. He pulled his friend along with him toward the girls.

"Hey, congratulations, ladies! Those are the most fantastic signs I've seen yet!"

The girls smiled.

"I'm Kevin Powell, chairman of the Youth for Crandles group," he smiled, offering a handshake. "What are your names?"

Thor noticed the girls trying to suppress laughter. Kevin continued with his line.

"I know Art Crandles, and he'd really like to see you with those signs at the meeting tonight."

The taller girl broke in. "You think these are for his campaign?"

"Why sure!" beamed Kevin as he admired the strands flashing "ART...ART...ART...." "And they look great on you both!"

"Are you off-line!" laughed her friend. "Take a close look."

She turned around. On the filament strands across her back, the word "ART" was rearranged. It now spelled "RAT."

"We're promoting a new show at the Acoustic Art Gallery. 'ART RAT RACE' is the exhibit," the girl explained. "And it just so happens that we're supporting Gwen Griffin!"

"Are you really youth chairman for Crandles?" the other asked.

Kevin gulped and nodded.

She turned to Thor. "Tell your friend he has my sympathy."

The putdown was complete. The girls walked away laughing. Thor saw, that from behind, the change of "ART" into "RAT" was obvious. So, too, was Kevin's embarrassment.

"Sometimes I should keep my mouth shut."

"Can I tell Pam you said that?"

"Only if you want your circuits pulled out."

They continued together along the sidewalk to the next intersection. Kevin proceeded to the parking meter where he'd left his car and Thor crossed Binary Avenue to his father's office building.

Benson Data Consultants, or BenDaCon as it was more commonly known, occupied two floors and employed thirty people. The latest computing gear and state-of-the-art equipment had attracted the brightest workers and many major contracts. The current assignment, Election Data Processing Supervision, had brought the full staff into service. As a result, Thor had an opportunity to work on smaller jobs.

"Your father is in a vidiconference," said one of his secretaries. "I'll let him know you're here."

"Thank you."

As the boss's son, Thor was treated very well. He had, however, also established his own credentials. Thor's computing knowledge and expertise had earned him the respect of the company's full-time specialists. They recognized his genius and enjoyed his curious nature.

Three huge leafy plants disguised a junior workstation. A computer bank, a keyboard, a monitor, and multiplex drivers occupied the low desk, a VistaPhone outlet stood nearby. Thor pulled up his chair and studied the daily postings.

"One, two, four, eight, sixteen," he muttered, counting the entries. "Sixteen stores with defective At-Home Shopping services. The rate is increasing exponentially."

He pressed the computer storage drum into action. Further details came onto the twelve windows of his display monitor.

"At this rate, Stanton could have every store and bank closed in a few hours," he concluded. "Why is the system crashing?"

A check run on the Stanton Gift Boutique showed that his earlier purchase had not registered. The data had somehow slipped through the company's sales records. Fortunately though, customers' banking codes remained. This permitted the store to call through the bank computer and contact the customer. Orders could be confirmed, but the system was inefficient.

"RUN CHK RTN SWEEP," he entered, coding a checking routine sweep.

The fibre-optic cable lines carried the message to all the troubled user-computers. For the thousandth time, they went through their program files, input/output, searching for the gap.

"If we don't find this soon..." He hesitated to think what the end result might be.

The VistaPhone came on.

"Your father is between meetings, Thor," smiled the secretary. "He'd like to see you."

"In person or on this?"

"For real," came the response.

Before leaving the workstation, Thor touched another window gate on the computer screen. It ordered up a new command: "CHK: TRANSIENT DATA FLOW." This would run independently of all previous instructions.

"Have a seat," invited Edward Benson, as the youth entered the executive suite. The vidiconference was just ending. Below the camera which recorded Mr. Benson was a video screen showing the four other people involved, each in different cities. These privately transmitted meetings saved enormous amounts of time, energy, and money. They eliminated the hours spent traveling, hotel costs, and the exhaustion that often plagues business travelers. Executives could meet more frequently and conduct more business transactions through vidiconferencing than they ever could by physically hopping around the country.

".... and as soon as that is solved, we'll receive clearance?" asked Edward Benson as the televised meeting concluded.

"Only when that occurs," said one of the men on the screen.

They exchanged wishes and signed off. Mr. Benson rose from his chair and took off his jacket. Nearing middle age and greying slightly at the temples, he was a tall, sinewy man who retained the physique he'd developed playing college basketball. His dark blue eyes and fair hair were strikingly similar to his son's. Mrs. Benson often called one by the other's name.

"You look real tired, Dad."

"It's no wonder, with the hours and headaches coming from all these voting details. Did you recognize that last man speaking?"

Thor shook his head. They were all strangers to him.

"He's the federal supervisor for local elections. And do you know what he said?"

Again the boy shrugged.

"The whole country will be watching what happens in Stanton. This is the prototype. Why? This electronic voting day is a first for the nation, and if it's successful, the upcoming federal election will be decided by at-home balloting."

Thor already knew this was the way of the future. He also sensed the concern in his father's voice.

"Security is the one unknown factor."

The man said it with a shake of his head, which Thor recognized as a sign of frustration. The vidiconference must have raised the issue.

"National politicians will be watching us like hawks. Nothing can, nothing must, go wrong. The voting transmission signals are to be absolutely private, confidential, and secure. If not, democracy loses. And personally, since BenDaCon has the contract, so do we."

All the years Edward Benson had studied and struggled in business were now on the line. His eyes glistened with determination.

"How can I help?" asked Thor.

"By doing what you're already doing, son. And if I seem impatient or quick-tempered, you know why. It has nothing to do with you, or your mother. I hope you understand," he said softly. "I'm walking the tightrope until E-Day."

"So are a lot of people," offered Thor in consolation. "Kevin and Pamela aren't even talking to each other."

Mr. Benson laughed to relax himself. "Welcome to the wonderful world of adulthood!"

Thor grinned. His father seemed relieved to have confided in him. He had not spoken this long to Thor for nearly a month. Working to a deadline put so much pressure on the man that Thor wondered if it was all worthwhile.

"I'm checking the At-Home Shopping mess," replied the

boy in answer to his father's question about his current assignment.

"Ah, yes," intoned Mr. Benson. "The mystery of the vanishing purchases. What are you running?"

"A few things. Transient data checks."

"If it isn't a programming problem, you might have to get on your hands and knees to check every cable going through the system."

That was the ultimate solution. Of course, the man was really half-joking. The effort would be nearly impossible. Edward gave his son a reassuring pat on the back.

"Take it one step at a time," he advised.

Back at the junior workstation, the youngster rocked in his chair. The INPUT window on the computer display monitor was blinking. It was one of a dozen separate locations which handled assignments simultaneously. The INPUT address had priority. Thor released the waiting file.

"TRANSIENT DATA FLOW CHK COMPLETE," identified the program. "READ OR DUMP."

The instruction baffled the boy. Somehow the incoming data was conducting its own checks! Was something searching through the mainframe computer?

"READ, please," muttered the youth.

If he indicated the "DUMP" procedure, stored data would be erased. Thor had no idea what was threatened, should that occur. In the nanoseconds after ordering "READ," the screen came to life.

"Names, banking codes, and purchase orders," he mumbled.

The At-Home Shopping service was back in operation!

He ran a check on the Stanton Gift Boutique. It returned positive. There, in the midst of the afternoon purchase records, was the entry " PAMELA POWELL, WATERFORD VASE," with the product number, home address, and test banking code. The problem had been solved!

"But how did I do it?"

Before reporting the achievement to his father and the clients, Thor Benson realized he had to explain the solution to himself. And that gave him difficulty. For though he recalled his methods, there seemed no reason why the system had suddenly been restored.

Then, as quickly as the data had appeared, it vanished! Even the banking codes were wiped. Something seemed to be loose inside the system. Something was eating up the database!

He immediately took the rest of the At-Home Shopping program off-line. If a disruptive instruction was losing valuable data, Thor Benson was responsible for finding out where it was coming from.

"SEARCH ALL ENTRY CODES," he ordered.

Among the millions of active entries, the computer returned a list of the ten most frequently used codes. Two of them were identical.

"Getting hot," he whistled.

He recorded the strange entry code first, then punched back into the mainframe. He had no idea where this was going. In the suspenseful moment of waiting for the monitor to display new information, he could hear his own heartbeat.

"MEETING AT 1725 BINARY PARK WEST."

Thor stared at the message. Where did it come from? He put aside that question for the moment and concentrated on the contents. They made no sense. The lot numbers on Binary Avenue only went to the 1200 block. And there was no street called Binary Park West in Stanton. As he pondered the mystery, the VistaPhone screen lit up.

"Hi, Pam. What's life like out there?"

"Can't you see?" she asked, leaning to the side. The scene behind her showed the frenzy of Mayor Griffin's reelection headquarters. "This place is a madhouse."

"You're right at home."

"Thanks, Mister Hilarious. Are you coming to the meeting tonight?"

Thor felt dismayed. "Not with all this work. But maybe. What time is it starting?"

"1815."

Her response jolted his mind. He stared at the desktop computer monitor.

"1815?" he spoke slowly. "In real time, that's 6:15 this evening."

"I always said you were a genius," came Pam's sarcastic reply. "But this is an election campaign I'm working on, and there's no such thing as 'real time.' We're going twenty-four hours a day."

"So 1725 is really 5:25," Thor slowly repeated.

On the VistaPhone, Pam leaned into the fibre-optic relay lens. She pretended to examine his workstation area.

"What are you doing? Burning out?"

"Is there a park on Binary Avenue?"

"If there was, it would be blocking traffic."

"Pam, please. Is there a Park West anywhere on Binary?"

She responded to the earnestness of his questioning.

"No, nothing officially called a park." A moment of contemplation followed. "But there is that big sign on Binary, near the City Hall. The one that says 'Parking West, Parking East.'"

Of course, the main parking lot!

"Maybe I will see you at the meeting, Pam. Thanks!"

"Right. At 1815."

They waved to each other as the VistaPhones switched

off. Thor reread the strange message, then hit the PRINT button and tore out the hard copy paper. Next, he sent the At-Home Shopping service back on-line.

Thor had been waiting only a few minutes before he concluded that a parking lot was a miserable place to be standing around. Staying clear of cars was enough of a concern without having to wander in search of strangers meeting.

According to his wristband, the time was 5:24. He was standing near the entrance to the lot below the Parking West sign. Since it was the end of the working day, most traffic was leaving. In the far lane, he saw a white limousine come to a stop. A silver-haired man emerged from the car, a pair of sunglasses contrasting starkly with his light features.

Two other men climbed out of a nearby vehicle. Thor had noticed them earlier, moving luggage from the trunk to the front of the car. The silver-haired gentleman, Thor guessed him to be about sixty years of age, passed right by him.

The man approached the pair and shook hands. One of them lifted a black box from the front seat. The silver-haired man smiled, said something, and the others laughed.

Meanwhile, the white limousine had circled to wait in the vicinity. The silver-haired man picked up the black box and walked to his limo. As he did, the other men got into their car and drove away.

Thor Benson knew he would not sleep easily until he could identify the man and his car. What intrigued the boy most was the contents of that black box. He stepped forward to make his move.

Suddenly, he stiffened. A hand had gripped his arm!

CHAPTER 4
The Mystery Man

"Gotcha!"

He whirled around. "Pamela!"

"Now what are you doing...?"

Screeching tires interrupted her question. The white limousine sped from the parking lot to vanish in the rush-hour traffic. Thor kicked the ground in frustration.

"There it goes, right?"

"Right."

Though Pam felt responsible for interfering, she didn't admit it. Just maybe, she thought, she had prevented Thor from getting involved in something too dangerous.

"How did you get here?"

"When we talked on the VistaPhone, I could tell by your weird questions and the look on your face that you were up to no good. So I decided to join you."

"At least you're not 'just passing by.'"

"But I am. The candidates' meeting starts in an hour."

Thor shook his head as he smiled at the slender, dark-haired girl. There simply was no chance to avoid the issue with Pamela. The political campaign dominated her every waking moment.

"As long as we have the freedom to choose our government, it's our duty to participate," she insisted. "Think of those countries where people are jailed only because they want honest elections. We can't take democracy for granted!"

Thor couldn't argue with what she said. But even though he agreed with her, he didn't want to pursue the topic. He knew it would quickly lead them to the choice for mayor and who supported who.

"Is the Stanton Gift Boutique nearby?"

"What are you getting me?" she asked without missing a beat.

"A few minutes of browsing."

As it happened, the store was two blocks from the parking lot. They strolled in that direction while talking about the Powell family's plan for a summer vacation.

"Not another computer camp!" she declared, referring to the location of an earlier MicroKidz adventure. "At least not this year. Mom was thinking of some tropical island. Skin diving for coral, bright sandy beaches, and lots of palm trees."

"Sounds like a postcard," Thor commented.

"Maybe you could come along with us."

Her suggestion was not farfetched. Thor certainly had the funds to pay for his own vacation. This financial security came from sales of a home laserdisc video game he'd developed with his father. Sales of *Starbryte* had been phenomenal for almost a year. His parents had helped him establish a trust fund for future use, while some money was set aside to buy equipment for his workshop, treat friends on nights out, and spend on holidays. "I have enough money to buy a new car, but I'm not old enough to get a license," he once told a media reporter.

The Stanton Gift Boutique was on a laneway that ran off

Binary Avenue. Tourists found it a pleasant area to hunt for souvenirs; the people of Stanton preferred to use the store's video catalogue for At-Home Shopping.

Pamela went in while Thor lingered at the front window. He surveyed the display merchandise scanned by video cameras. This was the same image customers first received when tuning in at home.

While Pam examined a few store items, Thor approached the manager's office. A peek through the open door showed the older man leaning over his video sales computer.

"It's about time something was done!" the manager appealed once Thor had introduced himself. "Half my sales are lost, the other half are not going to the right customers. It's a complete shambles!"

Thor tried to calm the man by explaining that the problem was nearly solved. "Just a few bytes away."

"But I keep receiving wrong codes or no locations," the manager continued in disgust, ignoring Thor's joke. "Things that don't add up. Some have nothing to do with my store."

"Can you point one of them out?"

The manager produced a sheaf of printout papers. He indicated a series of numbers that were entered below customers' names and orders.

"And I have no idea where these things come from. It's almost as if someone had broken into my office, written out the names of customers and their banking codes, then went out and stole that money!"

Alerted by the shouting, Pamela walked to the office.

"Someone is stealing their money?" Thor asked in disbelief.

"Yes! Just by taking the customers' financial transaction codes!"

"Why haven't you told us this before?"

"But I have!" stated the irate man. "Twice today!"

Thor had trouble believing that. Only when the manager pulled a copy page from his printer did the truth strike hard. There was a data snatcher in the At-Home Shopping system!

"Didn't you see this message? I TeleMailed it 'URGENT'. Directly to BenDaCon!"

No, Thor had not received the notice. If the company had, he would have been notified. In fact, Edward Benson would have personally taken control. The notice had surely been intercepted.

"This is my livelihood," continued the store manager. "My business is being destroyed by people I can't even see!"

A bitter lesson was unfolding. The At-Home Shopping service, which had saved many failing businesses, was being sabotaged. While the older man gave other examples, a bell sounded above his computer to register an incoming message.

"See if anything happens," he invited the youngsters.

They watched the customer's name, choice of item, address, and banking code appear on the display screen.

"Get that printed!" Thor ordered.

A touch of the PRINT button made an instant hard copy of the purchase order. He got it just in time.

Suddenly, a series of numbers popped onto the display monitor directly under the customer's personal data!

"Let's get that too!"

He was too late. Before Thor could activate the printer, the screen went blank. All reference to the purchase had vanished.

"We've just witnessed a robbery," Thor said to the others. "No guns, no threats, no getaway car—a clean job."

"Should we call the police?"

"Give us a day," Thor requested from the man. "In the meantime, sign off the At-Home service. You may lose some business, but at least you won't lose the whole store."

The manager agreed. He escorted the youngsters onto the street. They spoke for a moment about the mysterious occurrence. His parting comment awakened the couple to the possibility of something they hadn't thought of before.

"I own a little store, and you saw how easy it was for a computer break-in. Now we're having this election for mayor and a referendum. At-Home voting. I wonder if it's just as easy for someone to control that?"

Thor knew that it was but didn't say so. The technology was available on the black market. But why would anyone bother with a small-town election for mayor?

Pamela answered his question later as they sat together by the City Hall fountain discussing the evening's events.

"Because it's the first time electronic balloting will happen in this country. And if someone can crack the voting codes here, they'd be able to control national elections!"

Her words sent a shudder through them both. The peaceful setting heightened their fears. As evening sunlight reflected off the windows, an inner darkness swept through the couple. Even the flag hung limp against the pole, with no breeze to raise it. Was some invisible foe threatening the democracy they'd always taken for granted?

"Almost time for the candidates' meeting," Pamela sighed. "I wonder if it makes any difference now."

"Let's not think the worst."

She braved an optimistic smile.

Kevin Powell had smiled continuously for the past two hours. He had also shaken at least two hundred hands. He was beginning to feel like a real politician.

"Hi! Great to see ya! Here, take a button! They have

flashing microdots! Hold up your sign higher when Art arrives."

Kevin's job as youth chairman had many facets to it. He trained canvassers, wired and posted election signs, compiled data lists, and programmed VistaPhones. On this evening, he'd organized a floor demonstration. Mainly, he took charge of getting the young people involved. Art Crandles's policies promised a lot to the youth. Since the majority of Stanton's citizens were under twenty-five, it was hardly a surprising commitment.

"And when he comes out, make lots of noise!" Kevin told a group of supporters near the front. "Loud applause, cheering, whistling! Let's give the press something to televise."

"What do we do when the mayor speaks?" asked a girl.

"Nothing. Gwen Griffin has her own cheering section," he snickered. "But we have the best seats! Because we have the best man!"

His pep talks had worked. The auditorium was filled to capacity within the hour and the prime locations were held by supporters of Crandles. Flashing posters dominated the scene. The atmosphere was truly electric.

The Griffin supporters were less organized. Many of these people were older and more reserved in their enthusiasm. It was Gwen Griffin's plan to campaign on her past successes. She considered ultraflashy displays, smooth packaging, and slick speeches deceptive; they might be fine for a soap salesman, but not for a government leader.

When the mayor was introduced onstage, the applause was polite. The reaction to Crandles's entrance, however, showed the effect of precision planning. An unaware visitor would guess that the President himself had arrived.

"Sssshhh!" Kevin silenced some co-workers who

became restless when the moderator began her opening remarks.

Kevin left the front seating section to check on other groups. As he made his way around the room, he saw two familiar figures leaning against the rear wall. He worked his way over to them and, before they knew what was happening, pinned tiny, flashing CRANDLES buttons onto their shirts.

"Thanks for nothing," Pam said as she returned it.

"Still sitting on the fence?" Kevin asked Thor.

"And enjoying the view."

The three friends stood together as the speeches began. First to the podium was Mayor Griffin. She outlined the healthy progress Stanton had made during her term of office and revealed her future plans for a new housing complex, tax breaks for high-tech firms, increased daycare facilities, and more assistance to the elderly.

"Stanton is a great place to live, and with your support, together, we will continue to make it better!"

What Gwen Griffin lacked in forceful delivery, she made up for with honesty. Dressed in a bright, stylish outfit, the mayor projected a wholesome charm. Her soft reassuring voice gave her speech a quality that exceeded the message. Many people felt very comfortable with her.

Kevin, however, was not impressed and he let his feelings be known to Pamela and Thor when the mayor finished.

"She was okay last time, but dull. This year she's not as okay, and even more dull."

"That's informed political analysis?" hissed Pam.

"No, my gut reaction."

"Just where your brains are, Kevin."

Thor saw the confrontation heating up and stepped between them.

"For the last time, give each other a break!" he whispered, trying to avoid attracting attention.

Applause following the mayor's speech drowned out the heated exchange. Tears glistened in Pamela's eyes. Kevin stomped away.

Thor put his arm around Pam to comfort her. Hurt feelings and a divided family angered him. This had to be resolved, Thor Benson told himself, and soon.

"...Mister Art Crandles!"

Thunderous cheers greeted the candidate. The excitement of his introduction would be hard to maintain. But his supporters were well rehearsed and gave the national news a boisterous show of support to televise.

As Crandles began to speak, Thor caught sight of the silver-haired man moving along the sidelines.

"Wait here, Pam."

Thor stepped into the aisle where the man stood. At close range he appeared to be younger than sixty, the round glasses giving him the appearance of a sporty businessman. His silver hair remained the man's most notable feature, positively identifying him for Thor.

Thor wondered why such a person would attend this meeting rather than watching it on cable in the comfort of his home. As he studied the gentleman, thoughts of the earlier encounter came to mind. He recalled the strange time code message he'd picked from the computer terminal that led him to witness the man receiving that black box in the parking lot.

Art Crandles was speaking about his plans for Stanton. His words went unnoticed by Thor whose attention was riveted on the silver-haired man. He was taking notes now, an action that seemed peculiar for someone who did not in any way resemble a news reporter.

When the candidate's silky speech ended, the anticipated ovation followed. Thor also leaped to his feet, not to cheer for Crandles, but to keep track of the mysterious gentleman.

A crush of bodies surged toward the stage. Thor lost sight of the man. A glance above the crowd to the back of the auditorium was discouraging. Pamela had also gone.

A side exit door stood open. The cool night air was too inviting to resist. As he came outside with the other worn-out audience members, his eyes lit up.

Parked by the stage door exit was the white limousine!

"Now I've got you," he chuckled to himself.

The silver-haired man moved quickly from the building. A chauffeur opened the rear door, the man bent over and slid inside. Several people followed the mystery man into the car.

With a shock, Thor recognized the last person climbing into the white limousine.

It was Kevin Powell!

CHAPTER 5
A Mixed Display Menu

A Stanton Police car was parked in the Powell driveway.

"Want me to go in with you?" Thor asked Pam as they neared.

"No, thanks."

He feared the worst. Thor had not mentioned where he'd last seen Kevin. The departure in the white limousine had left him stunned. Against his better judgment, he'd decided to remain silent.

For her part, Pamela had had a pleasant time. The candidates' meeting had gone well, and she'd managed to spend an evening with Thor.

"I'll give you a call in the morning, all right?"

He watched Pam walk up to her front door, then jogged across to his own house.

"Hi, Mom! Long time no see."

"No hear, either. Two men in the house and I still eat dinner alone. You should have called earlier, Thor."

"I didn't know how long we'd be. Sorry."

"Your father hasn't left the office. More of that election business. How was your day?"

Thor gave his mother a summary while he prepared a fast dinner for himself. Laraine Benson was a few years younger than Edward, who had been her college sweetheart. The green track suit she wore was actually her business outfit; Mrs. Benson was a trainer at the Flexercise Center. The woman's relaxed attitude contrasted with her husband's recent frenzy.

"Is Dad under too much stress?" Thor asked, when he sat down opposite her.

"Not any more than he's handled in the past. But he has been burning the candle long into the night, and that's not good. I've told him to slow down," she confessed. "Everything about this electronic voting is giving him headaches."

"Me too," mumbled the youngster.

While his mother blended fruit juice shakes for them, a bell tone rang in the hallway. Thor stepped out to see the image of Pamela come onto the VistaPhone.

"That was quick. Saying good night again?"

She did not seem happy to see him. "Could you please come over here, Thor?"

"Right now?" he asked uneasily.

With a quick excuse to his mother, the boy ran out of the house and across the street.

The Stanton Police car was still parked in the Powells' driveway. Thor thought again of Kevin and tried to imagine all was well with his friend.

"Sergeant Dalby," he said in a quiet greeting.

The police officer wagged his head. He had known the Powells and Bensons for years and was on good terms with everyone. In previous adventures, the sergeant had helped the MicroKidz to confront and arrest lawbreakers. This evening, though, he spoke sternly to Thor.

"Can you explain this?"

The police officer thrust a computer printout sheet at the boy. Circled on one column was the name "PAMELA POWELL, WATERFORD VASE."

"From the Stanton Gift Boutique?" asked Thor.

"So you do know after all," grumbled the officer.

"That isn't my bank code," Pam insisted. "I told you I knew nothing about it."

"She's right, Sergeant Dalby. That's my mistake."

Mrs. Powell spoke up. "Then you owe Pamela an apology. And an explanation."

It took Thor a few minutes to explain the situation. He admitted using the girl's name, but only for a program checking routine. He believed that the data had been erased along with all the other listings. In fact, Thor remembered seeing it being wiped from the computer screen.

"As a matter of course, I'll check with your father," Sergeant Dalby concluded. "When I received this sheet at the station, I knew there was some crazy reason behind it. Or else someone was trying to set Pam up."

The officer was satisfied with Thor's story. Since the youngsters had a reputation for solving numerous high-tech mysteries, Thor's explanation was consistent and credible.

"By the way," said Sergeant Dalby on the way to the door, "that propane explosion must have been a barnstormer."

Thor squinted. "How did you find out?"

"From Hines, the aviation investigator. He dropped into the station with the report. I saw you and Kevin listed as witnesses."

"You sure get around, Sergeant."

"That's just what I was going to say about you kids," laughed the officer. "Anyway, they think the fire started because of the forced landing. The pilot didn't want any evidence left."

Pamela broke in. "What evidence?"

"Whatever they were smuggling, I don't know. It's really out of our jurisdiction."

"Smugglers? In Stanton?"

Sergeant Dalby turned from the youngsters toward Mrs. Powell. She appeared very concerned at the disclosure.

"Nothing to worry about, Kay. Those aviation people are handling it all."

His words did little to put her at ease. After the policeman left, Thor and Pamela followed her into the living room. She wanted to hear all about the incident.

Thor spoke easily and calmly to Mrs. Powell. In the years they had lived on Matrix Boulevard, the families had shared many experiences. The most painful was the divorce period after Mr. Powell abandoned his wife and two children. Although Kay must have retained some bitterness, she kept it from Kevin and Pamela. She rebuilt her life and established herself as a highly regarded math instructor at Stanton High School.

"Mom, there's nothing to worry about."

"You can say it, Pamela, but I feel differently. Look at the time. Kevin isn't home. He hasn't even called."

Thor remained silent.

"I saw him at the meeting," Pam reassured her. "He's probably working back at the Crandles headquarters."

"Well, the least he could do is call and say so."

The discussion ended as Mrs. Powell left the room. Classes in adult education were scheduled the next day and she had lessons to prepare. Thor wished her good night.

Pam walked him to the side door. "Sorry for the false alarm."

"Hey, I'm the one that owes you the apology. I really did see that data get erased. But somehow it popped back in."

She gave a coy smile. "Things are like that."

Moments like these left him feeling uncertain. Whistling nervously, he wandered back across the street. The brightly shining stars were magnificent tonight, and Thor stopped to admire the sky before he went in.

While he stood watching, a car drove down the street and pulled up in front of the Powell house. Thor looked on from the shadows as its single passenger climbed out.

Kevin had returned.

At BenDaCon, the staff maintained an intensive schedule examining additional program routines. Nothing would be permitted to upset the detailed election plans. Before E-Day, the entire fibre-optic relay system had to be completely secure.

Edward Benson arrived with his son while the morning was still dark. The last time Thor had been up so early was for a fishing trip. In a way, this too was like fishing: searching the communications network for an illegal entry.

"It might be easier to hunt shark with a net than to do this," Mr. Benson said dryly.

Tension increased as the remaining staff filtered in. Many had left just a few hours before, returning home for a short sleep and change of clothing. The deadline was upon them, and Thor took his place at the junior workstation.

"Call in the team," Edward advised his secretary.

The assembly took place in his office. Some of Stanton's brightest computer analysts were among the group. Mr. Benson began the meeting with a review of events.

Thor had not been invited, but he watched the proceedings on the inter-office VistaPhone. His other assignments were put on hold. The boy was more intrigued with the specialists' meeting.

"Each registered voter has a Personal Authorization Code," Edward was saying. "This P.A.C. can be used only once, prior to entering a ballot choice. We believe that our present security measures are adequate."

"Is that enough?" asked one woman.

"It is, since we'll go on line with a modified version of our corporate call-back safety routine. For instance, the voter dials his P.A.C. In the nanoseconds before he continues, our mainframe computer has checked if that voter is indeed registered. It then disconnects that person temporarily. Program Two is activated and dials the P.A.C. Thus, the person who entered it casts his ballot. Secretly and securely."

"How long does it take?" asked the same woman.

"We have it down to .08 seconds."

"It's not fast enough," chuckled one man.

"We're all trying our best," smiled Edward.

"And the referendum?" inquired a recently employed young lady.

Thor knew about the referendum. Before voters selected their choices for mayor and members of the town council, a list of twenty questions would be presented. This referendum dealt with matters such as local taxes, school reform, housing, road widening, social services, business bylaws, and zoning rules. It had not received as much notice as the race for mayor, but the referendum was just as important. People had the opportunity to voice their opinions on individual issues.

"Many politicians believe that the next stage of democracy rests with referendums coming from citizens' homes," continued Edward Benson. "Since this is also a first for Stanton, you realize the additional pressure created."

Thor turned off the inter-office VistaPhone. He felt alienated from the real excitement. Though his father's company was supervising the data processing for the election, he was excluded from the action. His two best friends were working on political campaigns which were off-limits to him. He had work to do, but it made him feel useless because he wasn't making any headway with it.

"Who cares about this At-Home Shopping mess?" he muttered.

But the job had to be done.

"Let's run it again," he sighed.

While he worked, events from last evening kept coming back to him: the strange appearance of the silver-haired man in the parking lot and at the meeting, Kevin's departure in the white limousine, his late arrival home. Then there was the dream he'd had during the night: he was standing alone inside the Stanton Gift Boutique with thousands of complaining customers. What a nightmare!

"So where did the problem go?" he asked himself.

Today, every client on the At-Home service had reported "business as usual." The system was functioning perfectly. Although Thor tried to find a data leak, all tests returned safe and secure.

"It's clear now, Dad."

"Good thing, son," he smiled over the VistaPhone. "But there's a problem with the local TeleMail network."

Thor groaned to himself. "What's wrong?"

"A glitch in the routings." Edward noticed his son was not thrilled by the report. "Everyone else is working on the election. I've no spare staff."

Thor knew where his duty lay. "I'll get right on it."

A moment later, however, when he started onto the TeleMail stint, the old feeling resurfaced.

"Why don't they just junk this and start from scratch?" he wondered angrily.

Electronic mail sometimes caused more problems than it solved. The old stamp-and-letter system had been replaced by direct data transmissions which had one major drawback. In the past, a bag of mail was occasionally delayed or misplaced. Now, one false entry at TeleMail Central could erase millions of private messages from existence. To the computers, personal letters were simply random bits and bytes.

Two corporations had filed complaints. Their outgoing TeleMail was not reaching the proper terminals. Every code address had been checked, but the breakdown remained. What was wrong?

"Guess I'll plug in and watch for awhile," Thor decided.

The REM Corporation did research work for advertising agencies. A prominent Stanton firm, REM used the TeleMail system for ninety percent of its business dealings. As a result, very little was being done today.

"Surveys. Accounts payable. Business replies."

Each section was operating independently. Yet the transfers showed only a negative output. Thor scanned the main TeleMail circuits for any irregularities.

Two hours went by. He had found nothing using standard tests.

"I'm beat!" he yawned aloud.

He was also hungry. He needed food and a fresh air break. In one last effort, Thor set the REM Corporation circuit into a double duty role. He would try to set up lunch and see if there was a systems response.

"MEMO: PAMELA POWELL AT MAYOR GRIFFIN CAMPAIGN H.Q. RE: LUNCH 1205 BURGERS C.O.D.," he typed onto the monitor.

Still chuckling, he sent the message by TeleMail. It was a simple send-receive mode test. Even though it went out on the REM Corporation line, Pamela would know who sent it. The time-code clue was one reason. The other was that only one boy took her out to lunch for burgers.

"RECEIVED. CONFIRMED MEMO. REM CORP. 8-322 c."

It had worked! The message had come back more slowly than normal, but that was probably because it was the first of the day.

Thor stopped by the executive office on his way out. His Dad was involved in another vidiconference, so he left a message with the secretary to tell him that one of the TeleMail links had been cleared.

"Still some time before the 1205 lunch," Thor thought. "Great day for a walk along Binary."

Another cloudless day was giving Stanton the opportunity to draw its energy needs from solar power collectors. These multipanels had been installed at various locations around town. The energy they obtained from the sun was safe and reliable. It was also free. The system had become a campaign issue in this election because the equipment required an overhaul to restore it to peak efficiency, and for some reason, Art Crandles opposed it. One rumor was that he hated the system because Mayor Griffin had installed it. Others said he wanted to experiment with new methods of burning fossil fuels. Neither made much sense to Thor.

A crowd had gathered outside Mayor Griffin's reelection offices. Four men were unloading a delivery truck. Roars of laughter swept through the sidewalk assembly. At first, Thor thought they were reacting to a shipment of humorous posters or costumes. As he got closer though, his nose told him differently.

He squeezed through the crowd. Standing in front of the offices was Pamela Powell, close to tears as she argued with a deliveryman.

"There it is! Plain as the day!" shouted the man, holding an order form in his hand. "Received, confirmed, C.O.D. Cash on Delivery!"

The aroma wafting from the boxes was unmistakable. Obviously, a terrible misunderstanding had occurred.

"Thor! Help me out!" Pam called.

"I've got it here," insisted the deliveryman. "Hot, fresh, and waiting to be paid for!"

"But why would I order one thousand two hundred and five hamburgers?" Pamela shouted back at the man.

This was not the lunch invitation Thor had intended.

CHAPTER 6
Dirty Tricks

"One thousand hamburgers!"

"That's a round figure, Dad."

"Where are they now?"

"Eaten. I had them sent to schools, parks, company plants," explained Thor. "Good thing it was lunch hour."

Edward stared in bewilderment at his son. This latest event was beyond reason.

"I admit sending the message, but something happened along the way," the boy continued. "Whoever has been poking through the At-Home Shopping service was also going through that TeleMail port, I'm sure of it. They saw my message coming through and added some bytes of their own that directed it to the catering company."

"Still, that's an incredible order! Why didn't they stop it?"

The youth shrugged. "The caterer thought it was food for the mayor's rally."

Time to digest the situation, thought Edward Benson. He leaned up against the large window in his office. Below him stretched the town of Stanton, its peace threatened.

"Dirty tricks," mumbled the man.

"What's that?"

"Nasty political games. Trying to destroy your opponent's image with foulups. In the past, ruthless people have tried to win elections by destroying their rival's reputation," said Edward in disgust. "I thought that was all left behind."

"Have there been other incidents lately?"

The man nodded. However, for security reasons he couldn't give his son any details.

"Leave it to us," Edward advised. "Take a break from work. If I need backup on election day, I'll call you in."

"Thanks, Dad."

"By the way, I took care of the catering bill."

Thor smiled gratefully. His father had one final word of advice.

"But the next time you ask Pamela to lunch, do it privately."

Every time Kevin Powell checked the voting registration lists, more names appeared. He wondered where these people were living. Their RESIDENCE code was in a category listed "STANDBY."

"Where are they all standing? In a field?" he wondered.

At least these names declared support for Art Crandles. In fact, all the voters listed on these floppy diskettes were for Crandles.

"TOP SECRET, CONFIDENTIAL," read the label on the side.

As youth chairman, and because of his skill with data systems programming, Kevin had access to numerous diskettes. The campaign manager trusted this youngster to help organize and register the Undecided Voters lists. He was sworn to secrecy.

"What's the latest estimate?" asked an aide.

"We're behind by 15 percent."

"Can we close the gap?"

Kevin waved his arms. "Do birds fly?"

"I asked a serious question," stated the assistant, an older man not accustomed to electronic voting calculations.

"By election day, those figures will be reversed," Kevin promised.

The man glanced over the computer assembly the boy operated. It remained a mysterious entity to him. He wondered whether these things were really necessary. Whatever happened to the good old days of knocking on doors, having coffee with the candidate, and marking your ballot in pencil with an X?

"Gone the way of the pet rock," he shrugged.

More data made its way onto the diskettes. Kevin continued to transfer the results from the last election in a street-by-street analysis. This identified where Mayor Griffin's support lay. Using that information, field workers could concentrate on those areas to campaign for Art Crandles.

"Keep up the good work, kid," said a voice from behind.

Kevin turned around to see the silver-haired man standing behind him. His dark suit and glasses contrasted starkly with the appearance of the rest of the workers. The man did not smile as he peered over the boy's shoulder at the display monitor.

"Thanks, sir. We're looking great."

After the silver-haired man walked away, Kevin resumed his program analysis feeling happy that his efforts were appreciated.

The "Hamburger Bungle" produced an unexpected result. News reporters and journalists flocked to Mayor Griffin's reelection headquarters for details. Because of her part in the affair, Pamela Powell was the main interview subject.

"It was a mistake, really," she tried to explain.

"But you donated the food to schools and people in parks," a reporter pressed. "Was that a mistake?"

"Not at all, we had to share it."

"This giveaway," prodded another journalist. "Was taxpayers' money used in the payoff?"

"No, it was a private donation."

"Will you admit this was really a wacky publicity stunt?"

Pamela stared back at the reporter. She winced, as though falsely accused of some crime. Words tumbled from her lips. The glare of the camera lights above so many peering faces brought on a dizzy sensation. Pam backed off, apologized, and left the gathering.

One of the mayor's assistants took over the press conference. She had more experience in dealing with the media. She praised Pamela for acting in the correct manner. Even the mayor was proud of the girl's actions, she told the press.

Meanwhile, the pressure mounted. There was no escaping the reporters. When Pamela came out of the office later, they were still there. The flurry of questions resumed.

"Please, can't you change the subject?" she asked. "Mayor Griffin has more important things to represent. There's the future of Stanton to consider, and why she's the best person to work for it."

"We can get that speech anytime," a reporter answered back. "This is news! It's different, offbeat. Something unusual, right?"

The message was clear and a lesson for Pam. To get press coverage like this, you had to have an angle.

Pamela wondered how that applied to slanting news reports.

That evening, Matrix Boulevard became an electoral battleground. Lawns sprouted a variety of signs. There were elaborately flashing posters lit by fibre-optics, and some that were more discreet and traditional. Supporters for each candidate visited the residents. They tried to win over the undecided and find out each voter's preference.

"Sorry, but we can't allow that," Laraine Benson said to requests for planting an election sign on her lawn. "We have to remain impartial."

"Just tell me if you've made up your mind to vote?" asked the insistent canvasser.

"Sorry, but I..."

"You're undecided, lady?" he interrupted.

Mrs. Benson studied the young man standing at her doorway. A beeping microdot button displayed Mayor Griffin's face smiling oddly.

"Does the mayor tell you to harass people?"

"Just to get the facts. Quick as we can," replied the young man with a laugh.

"Well, these are the facts!" Mrs. Benson tried to control her anger. "Who I support and vote for is my own business. And I don't appreciate your rude behavior!"

The words had no effect on the canvasser. "Still undecided?"

Mrs. Benson was not undecided; she was outraged.

"If you can't make up your mind, maybe this will help."

The young man thrust a pamphlet into the woman's hands. She was too stunned to refuse it. But she did react. Mrs. Benson crumpled the pamphlet bearing Gwen Griffin's photo.

"Who was that, Mom?"

Laraine Benson shook her head in disbelief. Her son asked again what had occurred.

"If Gwen Griffin wants to lose the election, she's doing all the right things," said the irritated woman. "I can't believe the rudeness of her workers. That's the third person today who has come by on her behalf. And they're all just short of insulting!"

This came as a surprise to Thor. Normally, canvassers were polite and courteous. After all, they represented their candidate and had to make a good impression.

"That sure doesn't seem right," Thor said to himself. "Why would the mayor's workers try to upset voters?"

He followed his mother to the family room. Mrs. Benson had assembled a new fitness program for her classes and wanted her son's reaction. A videotaped insert began the session. On the screen, two human forms appeared. Infrared close-ups featured parts of the body where heat loss took place.

"That shows the calories burning off," she explained.

Each exercise had a different rate of heat loss. As a result, persons wanting to lose weight and gain better muscle tone would know which was the most effective exercise to apply to that part of the body.

"Looks pretty fine so far," Thor said.

The images on the screen kept changing color fields. Near the end of the second section, they heard the front door closing.

"What a surprise! Ed's home early."

Laraine stepped out to greet her husband. A scowl had replaced his usual smile. He pointed out the front window.

"Who said that could be put up? Thor, come out here."

Laraine had pulled back the curtain to reveal a flashing sign on their lawn that declared, "WE SUPPORT MAYOR GWEN."

"Not me, Dad. That's the first I've seen of it."

His wife recounted the attitudes of the evening's canvassers.

"And I told that last young man we did not want a poster," she repeated. "What nerve!"

"It's against my contract regulations," Edward reminded them. "We can't show any favoritism. Somebody is trying to cause trouble."

Mr. Benson appeared exhausted. He had to go back to the office shortly. The preelection data input analysis demanded closer inspection. He asked his son to remove the sign from the lawn.

While Thor was pulling it loose, he noticed something odd. The photograph of Gwen Griffin was slightly distorted to make it appear that the mayor was winking slyly. An uncomplimentary image, he thought.

He hung the election poster over a hole in the wall of his workshop. It seemed fitting.

"How's Mr. Chips?" he asked.

The domestic robot stood guard silently. Since Thor was in town so much, he had not used it recently. He pressed the microcontrol panel for a test. The robot responded by turning in circles.

"Just how I feel," the boy thought.

The presence of his own computing equipment made him feel like working again. How could he use it to tie in with the mainframe at BenDaCon? It had already assisted in the earlier At-Home Shopping puzzle, but maybe he could upgrade its function. Perhaps it might be used to trace the missing data flow?

As the CREX+ microcomputer came to life, Thor entered the access code for his father's office. He requested the TeleMail location for outgoing data. Specifically, from both Mayor Griffin's and Art Crandles's campaign offices.

It was possible for Thor to monitor the TeleMail network because of his previous security clearance. The content of the messages remained private, but the addresses to which they were sent could be recorded.

"Put a line in the water and see what bytes," he punned aloud.

"Can I come in?"

The door opened, and Mr. Benson entered the workshop. He saw the computer screen displaying the TeleMail routes and smiled approvingly.

"I was just going to ask you to tap in there. Good thing we're on the same wavelength."

Thor had always had that feeling. There was a bond stronger than blood between the two.

"When are you going into town?"

"Shortly. I received a call about some unusual data transfers. The At-Home Shopping and TeleMail foulups are only part of it. No other locality has been affected," Edward added. "I believe there's some kind of a systems exchanger operating in Stanton."

The words fell on Thor with the impact of a blunt weapon.

"Aren't those things restricted? Illegal to import?"

"Yes, but all the same, one may have been shipped into the area. And with the upcoming election..."

Mr. Benson didn't need to elaborate on his unfinished statement. Thor realized that a terrible threat existed.

As his eyes wandered about the room, Mr. Benson's gaze came to rest on the newly hung poster of Mayor Gwen Griffin. From his point of view, the sly blink was obvious.

"That's a real mean shot."

"You'd think her campaign people could come up with something better," commented Thor.

After a closer look, Edward offered his own theory.

"I don't think the mayor or her people had anything to do with this."

Thor watched as his father lifted the poster from the wall. He switched on a laserscope and highlighted the area of the eye until the mayor's pupils glowed through the 3-D viewer.

"It's a microfilmed hologram," he concluded. "It's been made to give the effect that the mayor has a sleazy wink."

He focused the image under the laserscope 3-D viewer so Thor could observe the alteration for himself.

"More dirty tricks," said Mr. Benson. "I'm going to have this checked at Griffin's office. Do you want a ride into town?"

There was no resisting the invitation. The evening traffic had decreased and many pedestrians were strolling along the sidewalks enjoying the warm night.

"How about letting me off up there?"

"Fine. Give me a call if you want a lift back," offered Mr. Benson, as he stopped near a traffic light. "I'll be working for another three hours."

Thor waved goodbye, grateful that his father had not asked where he was going. He turned and walked toward Crandles's campaign headquarters.

He expected to find Kevin still on the job. He did not expect to find the white limousine parked out front.

"Well, a new volunteer!" Kevin yelled when he saw Thor. "I knew you'd want to join the winning side!"

Embarrassed, Thor shuffled over to his friend's workstation. Kevin sat surrounded by a number of floppy diskette packages, monitors, and two computer keyboards. The screens went blank as he sent the data into storage.

"Getting closer to E-Day," he smiled. "But we're positive."

"Are you? With sly winks and dirty tricks?"

Kevin seemed puzzled by the references.

"Come on, Kevin, you know what I'm talking about. You're a honcho, youth chairman! All those kids running around hassling people, planting weird signs of Mayor Griffin. You sent them out! Right?"

The expression on Kevin's face changed from disbelief to anger. He didn't answer the charges but called to someone across the room.

"Mr. Smyth?"

Thor turned to see the silver-haired gentleman approaching.

"This guy has some questions about our campaign," Kevin said sharply.

Thor felt suddenly uncomfortable.

"I'm the one to see in that case. My name is Ted Smyth. I'm the campaign manager for Art Crandles. What can I do for you?"

CHAPTER 7
Warning Trends

"Why didn't you tell the truth?"

"I did!"

Kevin Powell was challenging Thor. "No, you didn't!"

"I told Mr. Smyth he was running a very effective campaign," replied Thor. "Isn't that the truth?"

"But it's not what you said to me! You accused us of sabotage and harassment."

"Kevin, I was speaking to you alone. I've known you for years. Mr. Silver Hairs is a stranger to me. I didn't come to speak to him!"

They were hurrying down the street away from the campaign headquarters. Thor's surprise visit had upset Kevin's assigned schedule. The strain between the youths increased, every stride renewed feelings of discontent.

"When are you going to loosen up, Kevin?"

"After we win the election."

"What if you don't?"

"It's in the bag," he said confidently.

Thor wondered about the source of his confidence. Was Kevin spending too much time in front of the analysis screen? Were all the figures on voting tendencies taking their toll? Was the position of youth chairman going to his head?"

"How about a little bet on the final results?"

Now Thor was certain Kevin had reached a breakpoint. The only time his friend placed a bet was on a tab at the Big Byte.

"Okay," agreed Thor. "For what?"

"A year's supply of burgers!"

His added snicker was too much for Thor. The recent thousand-hamburger misadventure was still too fresh in his mind.

"I don't appreciate that."

"No hard feelings," chuckled the boy. He was trying to restore his own good humor. "Why don't we head over to the Byte?"

It was the best suggestion Kevin had come up with that day, even if his motivation was an old one; Kevin's appetite ruled his reason.

His sports car was parked at a nearby meter. Along the way, Kevin described an added benefit of working with Ted Smyth, the campaign manager.

"That white limo of his? You wouldn't believe what's inside it."

"A sauna and hot tub?"

"No, but there's enough room," Kevin went on. "There's a mobile computer facility! A console in the back has a VistaPhone, TeleMail port, keyboard microprocessor, modems, a printer. Even television!"

As the youth continued his insider's report, Thor relaxed a bit. Kevin had begun to speak to him in a less hostile way. Soon it felt like old times again.

The Big Byte offered lots of great fast food at low prices. Thick sandwiches and frothy fruit shakes were the house specialties. Located near Stanton High School, "The

Byte," as everyone referred to it, was a meeting place for the students. Where else, Kevin often said, could you enjoy a tasty snack while looking over the opposite sex?

They took a booth near the doorway. A video monitor on each table featured the daily menu. A customer made his choice and punched in the correct code. This registered electronically in the kitchen, the chef read the printout sheet and sent the order through.

"So when is Cheryl getting back?" asked Thor, after they'd ordered.

"Soon, I hope. Sure do miss her," Kevin said. "Absence makes the heart grow...how?"

"Fonder."

It was a good opportunity to relax. They munched on Kilobyte Klub sandwiches and watched the latest pop concert performances on the tabletop video screen. The charge for this micro-age jukebox was added onto the total bill.

Kevin tuned in the newest video by The Random Accessories. He thought it added a pleasant backbeat to his jaw cracking, a habit of his that unnerved Thor. The most influential musical group of the times, Accessories spoke out on behalf of their generation.

"I still like them," agreed Thor.

Tall yogurt shakes washed down the quick meal. Kevin flipped a coin to decide who paid. Once again, Thor had the honor.

The final bill for the food and music viewing appeared on the tabletop display monitor. Thor inserted his Automatic CashCard, verified his private account code, and pressed the TR button. In a nondescript building many miles away, the transaction entered a bank computer. Thor's debit became the Byte's credit.

They walked out into the plaza. Usually, they went to the

nearby Arkade to play laserdisc games, but they decided to pass on that today.

"How about going to a barbecue?"

"Kevin, are you bonkers? We've just eaten!"

"Not now. Tomorrow night. It's going to be a big event."

"A political barbecue?"

"Is there any other kind?" Kevin smiled. "All of the campaign people are invited. We can bring guests. It's out at the Crandles mansion. You've been there."

Thor recalled the visit. Kevin had driven there with Pamela and himself to pick up the floppy diskettes. It was on the way back that they'd witnessed the plane trouble and explosions.

"Has there been any update?" Thor wondered.

"Nothing. Maybe Hines and his aviation investigators have left town for bigger things."

They believed they'd heard the last of the incident. When Kevin dropped Thor off that night, he had the feeling that life was returning to normal.

"Sergeant Dalby?... What time is it?"

"Four o'clock."

Edward Benson opened the door to admit the police officer. The dark sky was still holding back the sunrise.

"A break-in?"

"A messy one," whispered Dalby.

Edward needed to hear the report twice before he was fully awake. "I'll get dressed and go with you," he said, tugging at his dressing gown.

The commotion woke Thor. Since he slept lightly, sounds such as car doors slamming on the street disturbed him. Laraine Benson often said his light sleeping was an indication that the boy's mind was always at work.

"What happened?" he mumbled from the hallway.

"Ssshh! Don't wake your mother," whispered Sergeant Dalby.

While his father got dressed, Thor heard the details of how BenDaCon had been vandalized.

"Punks, troublemakers," Sergeant Dalby confided. "Looks like they just wanted to wreck the place."

"Did the security cameras alert you?"

The policeman didn't answer. Tucking in his shirt, Edward rushed out of the bedroom. He spoke in low tones with Dalby as they left the house.

Watching the men depart in the police car, Thor sensed a surging hatred for the thugs who'd broken in to destroy his father's offices in a company he'd worked so hard to build.

As Pamela Powell drank her vitamin juice that morning, she noticed a blinking light atop the PIRX printer. A Tele-Mail message was awaiting transfer. Probably another memo from one of her mother's new students, she thought, clicking the machine on.

The girl returned to the kitchen, stretched for a moment and finished her juice. It had been a long, hard night at the mayor's reelection headquarters.

She tore the newly-printed message from the paper feeder and placed it on her mother's chair. Then she switched on the CompuNews service, bringing the latest world headlines onto the tabletop monitor.

Kevin came into the kitchen an hour later. His hair was still wet from showering.

There was a knock on the door and Thor let himself in. Kevin and Pamela, still in their pyjamas, looked up in bewilderment when he spoke impatiently to them.

"I thought you'd be ready."

Kevin wondered if he'd heard correctly. "Me? What do I have to be ready for?"

"The message! Didn't you pull it?" asked Thor.

Pamela reacted instantly by lifting the printout from her mother's chair and handing it to Kevin.

"Here, this one. I gave it to you earlier." She winked at Thor. "You know how slow he is in the morning."

"They want us there as soon as possible," said Kevin after reading the notice. "Something must have broken."

"Lots of things," Thor sighed. However, he didn't explain because the vandalism at BenDaCon was not to be revealed. Mr. Benson had insisted the break-in remain secret, ruling out any mention of it even to the Powells.

"What's up?" asked Pam. "Are you working with him for Crandles?"

Thor shrugged off the suggestion. Meanwhile, Kevin rushed from the room to dress. Pam had an opportunity to speak quietly with Thor.

"You know, it's been awhile since we went to a dance," she started hinting. "With all these final rallies and get-togethers, maybe we can find a party to go to."

"How about a barbecue party?" Thor asked, knowing there would be surprises all around. "But keep it to yourself, okay? Don't tell Kevin."

She agreed. Her brother entered the room just as the conversation ended. He had no inkling of what Thor had set into action.

"Tell Mom we're in town for a meeting, Pam. And I don't think I'll be back for dinner. Going out tonight."

"Who isn't?" she smirked.

The two youths drove through the morning rush hour, avoiding traffic delays by following the vehicle's R.T.A. This Route Travel Advisor received data from a central traffic computer. It relayed road conditions, traffic flow, tie-ups, accidents, and repair zones onto video maps in the dashboard. These units also displayed the car's location at all times, so that it was virtually impossible to get lost.

They parked outside the federal building. Thor followed Kevin into the elevator. They were both anxiously anticipating the encounter.

Mr. Hines greeted them.

"Your message worried us," admitted Thor.

"Are we really in danger?" Kevin asked.

"Let us say that you are at risk," replied the man. "A foreign investigation team came up with the records of our last meeting here. Your testimony was on those tapes."

"Who released them?" Kevin demanded.

"No one from this office, I assure you."

"Then how did they surface outside the country?"

"All our data was encoded 'CONFIDENTIAL AND PRIVATE.'" Hines explained the procedure. "It was sent to the Federal Aviation Investigation Board. Somewhere along the line it was intercepted."

"And the foreign link?"

"Smugglers."

"But of what?"

"Microtechnology. High-tech hardware that our country has import-export controls on," revealed Hines.

He led the youths to a viewing room near his office. A slide projector showed pictures of the abandoned airplane. Smoke wafted from the burning barn in the background. Close-ups of the scene after the fire was extinguished featured several strange containers.

"These packing crates were awaiting shipment," Hines said as he pointed to the container shells. "But after the plane got into trouble, the smugglers set off the propane tanks to destroy the evidence. As a result, nothing was shipped out on that plane."

"So the smugglers were foiled?"

"Unless they managed somehow to drop off materials," the man stated. "Something may have been unloaded."

"And recovered by that first helicopter we saw," Thor reasoned. "It picked up the shipment and the pilot crew right after the incident."

Hines warned the youths again of their situation. Because of the alert from foreign associates, the pair should be on the lookout for suspicious persons or activity.

"Especially with your reputations," Mr. Hines added. He was referring to previous media attention the MicroKidz had attracted. Their fame, he reminded them, did not guarantee their safety.

"We realize that, sir," Thor told him while they waited for the elevator. "But if there's anything we can do to get more information, we'll follow up on it."

They wished each other good luck and departed. On the way down, Kevin confessed his nervousness.

"Look what happens when we report an accident! Should have kept that cellular radio off!"

"How could we? Someone might have needed help."

"Who's going to help *us* when we need it?" Kevin raised his voice. "Smugglers play for keeps. I don't like it."

Thor didn't either, but, at the same time, he realized that they had a responsibility to act. In his mind, they had done the proper thing.

"I'm going into the campaign office," Kevin said, as they headed for the car. "Want a lift someplace?"

"No, I'll just stroll on to my Dad's." Thor hesitated to think what might await him there.

"I'll give you a call about the barbecue. Set the time and place to pick you up."

Thor remembered his own invitation to Pamela. He wanted the evening to be a surprise to both the brother and sister.

"Don't bother, Kev. I'll get there on my own. Working late."

They parted company. Thor stood to watch his friend drive off. With mounting dread, he climbed the steps to the BenDaCon building.

Two strangers were guarding the office entrance. A bulge in their jackets revealed that they were armed.

"Hey you! Kid! No entry!"

CHAPTER 8
Data Stacks and Party Snacks

The guard was not sympathetic, even though Thor explained his position. Fortunately, a BenDaCon employee came by, and he was finally admitted to the offices.

"Don't get upset," warned the staff member.

"Where is he?"

"Inside with the detectives. He's really taking it bad."

The reason quickly became apparent. Smashed pieces of computing equipment covered the floors. Plants, desks, and chairs had been overturned. The offices resembled the aftermath of a riot.

The boy sauntered over to his workstation. The terminal cable links were uprooted, display monitors smashed, and his carefully filed floppy disks soaked in oily fluids.

"Can I have a word with you?"

A detective had spotted Thor. His questions received only mumbled responses. Thor was in a state of shock.

"The sooner you tell me everything, the faster we can track down these vandals," prodded the man.

Before making any statements, Thor asked to see his father.

"Come along, then," said the detective.

The destruction appeared complete. Not an office or computer port had escaped damage. These vandals, there must have been several, had managed to escape BenDaCon's night security system. But how?

Edward Benson opened the door and gave his son a weary hug. They tried to console each other, both were so overcome by the catastrophe.

"How did they break in?" Thor asked incredulously. "The security cameras everywhere, noise detectors, remote surveillance... Did all that fail?"

"Somehow, it did. The detectives don't know themselves, son. But they will. This was sabotage!"

Before Edward continued his discussions with the government agents, he told his son not to make any statements. "That's our right. Wait until I'm with you, because I want to hear everything."

Making his way out of the building, the boy studied the racks of security cameras and laser tripwire detectors along the way. Why had they not functioned and alerted the police?

The staff reporting to Mayor Gwen Griffin's reelection headquarters this morning received a surprise. Four Stanton police officers guarded the front doors. A team of detectives was examining the premises.

"Is it a bomb threat?"

"Somebody said there was a break-in!"

"Where's the mayor? Is she safe?"

"Why don't they let us in?"

As the workers clamored outside, the rumors spread. Every question started another round of growing suspicions. The campaign volunteers became restless.

Pamela Powell arrived at her usual time. The crowd

remained on the sidewalk, blocking pedestrians. Her first thought was "another hamburger bungle."

"Just take an extended coffee break," one of the mayor's assistants told a group of workers.

An hour later, the detectives emerged from the building. A spokesman said the area was clear and safe to enter.

"But what happened?" everyone wondered.

"I'll speak to the mayor first," replied the officer.

After the police and detectives had left, the campaign workers filed into the headquarters. They found their offices in a very neat, tidy, and undisturbed condition.

"The place is cleaner now than when we left it last night," a few people remarked.

Pamela found her desk and working area in the same condition as she'd left it. Nothing seemed to have been tampered with, but an uncomfortable thought stuck in her mind.

She pressed the VistaPhone code for BenDaCon. Strangely, nothing happened. The company was out of the system.

"I'll send a notice to the workshop," she thought quietly, as she addressed a TeleMail notice to Thor.

Meanwhile, the campaign work shifted into the final stage. Election day was imminent. Last minute details required swift attention, an election-eve rally had to be organized.

"Thanks for your help, Pamela," said a soft voice.

The girl looked up from her desk into the warm eyes of Gwen Griffin. The mayor's appreciation was genuine. Gwen approached and exchanged kind words with all the staff. This charming, intelligent person, whose hairstyle and tennis skills sometimes received more notice than her civic work, stepped onto a chair in the center of the room.

"I know you are all asking the same questions and I'll

answer them just once," she began slowly. "The Stanton Police Department was on alert early this morning. Apparently, they believed these offices were to be vandalized." Anxious murmuring arose. "But, as you see, we fortunately escaped that threat. However, the concern has been raised. You know that election day is almost here, and to succeed we must intensify our efforts!"

While the mayor spoke, late arriving workers and assistants were briefed in whispers by their friends.

"Whoever planned to destroy these offices is very stupid! They don't know our organization! It's not a place. It's the people in the place!" Gwen Griffin maintained. "Vandals can't decide an election. That happens only one way; on the ballot. If everyone participates in a democratic way, then justice will triumph. The real losers are those vandals, those people who try to disrupt the order. Winning comes not through destruction, but through active discussion!"

Applause drowned out her final words of thanks. Her speech had achieved its purpose. People realized their earlier fears were unnecessary. The mayor's strength lay in her supporters, not in the security of a building.

Still, Pamela thought, if someone had broken into the offices last night, a great deal of destruction might have occurred.

"Not to the furnishings, but to the software!" she realized.

Although she differed with her brother on political choices, one factor linked them solidly: microtechnology. She was the youngest worker on the campaign who knew the complete details of the data system.

"I have to get inside there," she told herself.

This was not as easy as she'd hoped. The computer lines and data storage room had been closed by the investigators.

They advised that this off-line status continue until the noon hour.

"Please, I have to get in there," she pleaded.

The man who held the keys to the facilities hesitated.

"Only if you get the mayor's authorization," he said gruffly.

"If you recommend it, Pamela, I agree," Gwen Griffin said a few minutes later. "In fact, I wonder why that precaution was not already taken."

With the mayor's okay, the security guard unlocked the data storage room. He shook his head.

"I don't know where you kids get the nerve."

"You adults give it to us," was Pam's reply.

He stood by as the girl selected a number of floppy diskettes, mini-magnetic drums, and software registration files. After arranging the material, she pulled a suitcase from under a table. She loaded it up and lugged it through the office area. As she was passing through, one of the mayor's assistants called out to her.

"There's a call here from a Thor Benson, Pam."

"Tell him to hang on."

A taxi whisked her to 208 Matrix Boulevard. Thor was still lingering near the VistaPhone, waiting for her to call back. Her live appearance was very welcome.

"Are you moving in?" he asked looking at her suitcase.

"For two hours, if that's okay."

"What's up? Gwen Griffin kicked you out?"

"You wouldn't believe it if I told you," she said, beginning to recount the morning's events. The police on the outside, the detectives inside, the threat of vandalism, her fear that all the campaign tapes and disks might be sabotaged.

"Pam, I know just how you're feeling."

He did not elaborate. Instead, he cleared the workbench of everything but the CREX+ micro. He left it up to maintain its observation of the TeleMail lines.

"I need a lot of copying done as quickly as possible," she said.

Two diskette drives were capable of transferring data onto a new copy master. Thor pulled an old magnetic drum player from under the bench. It was one of several he'd bought in bankruptcy sales but hadn't used yet.

"Can't think of a better time than the present," he told her.

"Shouldn't you clean it first?"

"It's been in this dust protector since I got it. The only thing needed is power. And software!"

The workshop behind the garage soon resembled a miniature data processing and retrieval plant. Disks whirred, light indicators blinked, magnetic drums rotated, and test printout paper flowed.

"What are you doing with all the duplicates?"

"Storing them in a safe place."

"That's becoming a problem lately. Where do you think is safe?"

She pointed over to the lead-lined cabinet where Thor kept his private, most valuable disks.

He shook his head. "Check inside."

Pam bent over and opened the safe.

"It's empty!"

The dozens of special disks and added software which normally occupied the protective safe had vanished.

"Where are they?"

"Swallowed up."

Thor tried to get her to guess, but she was not in the mood for games.

"I told you, Pam. They've been eaten. And digested."

She waved a finger at him. "Are you still mad at me for that hamburger bungle?"

He moved over to Mr. Chips. The custom-built robot had remained by the doorway for the past few days guarding the workshop from intruders. More importantly, Mr. Chips now contained secrets of his own.

"Ready for a new trick?" Thor winked.

She watched him move the robot across the room. Pamela knew that the Bensons thought of the unit as a family pet. But teaching it new tricks?

"He's really getting smart," Thor continued.

A cable from an idle video display monitor was attached to the robot. Thor punched in a code sequence on its microcircuitry control panel. The robot didn't move.

"Well, so what?" Pam was getting edgy.

"Give him a bit."

A peculiar whirring sound came from the little robot, followed by three clicks. Suddenly, the blank display monitor began running program lists!

"Amazing," she whispered, watching Mr. Chips unload data stored inside his main compartment.

"Incredible, Thor. When did you do this?"

"Finished just a short while ago."

As the robot continued to unload the information, most of it Thor's high school exam disks, Pamela bent low to examine the connection. She was intrigued by this new use for Mr. Chips.

"Open it up," Thor suggested. "Press that latch forward."

This caused the front plate to slide across. It revealed the source of the data transmission. Two high-speed disk drums were stacked inside the robot's body. Rotating within these was the floppy diskette whose data filled the screen. Dozens of other disks were stacked in order, awaiting instructions.

"It's like a jukebox!" she exclaimed.

The container and stacked disks certainly did resemble an old jukebox that played 45 rpm records. In fact, Thor had gotten the idea from seeing such a machine. His parents often spoke about "dancing to music of the jukebox." He had asked what they meant, and one day Laraine Benson had taken him to an antique shop. Thor was enthralled by its playback method; as a result, he adapted the principle.

"I was thinking of new ways to reduce and store my disks," the youngster explained, "and to make the whole unit portable."

"You sure succeeded," Pam said admiringly. "Most people use these home robots for cleaning or security. Who would imagine that Mr. Chips is now a traveling data-bank?"

"Nobody, I hope."

It did not escape Pam's attention that Thor answered her question so quietly. She wondered what had motivated the invention of this unique retrieval system.

The experience at BenDaCon that morning had been a turning point for Thor. He realized how vulnerable all systems were to a determined criminal. Hardware could be smashed, software erased. By placing his most valuable disks inside the protective, lead-free, radiation-proof torso of Mr. Chips, part of the worries were eased.

He picked up the duplicate disks they'd copied for the mayor's campaign office. Without asking Pamela, he began sorting them into Mr. Chips's storage drum.

"Let's run a test to be sure everything's okay," he said.
"What do you want to check?"

Pam thought for a moment. She pressed the keyboard on

the microcontrol panel. Her instructions were clear: "LOCATE SUPPORTERS FILES. NAMES FROM 'E' TO 'G.'"

The front plate remained open. The couple leaned over to watch the SEARCH procedure in action. The diskettes whizzed, clicked, and loaded themselves into the drive.

"There it is," she smiled happily.

The video monitor displayed the file, listing all the members from EATON to GZOWSKI.

"Do you feel safe now?"

Pam patted the top of the robot. "Only with him."

Thor slid the front panel back into place.

"I still have to return these master copies," she said afterwards. "And I have some more work to do, but I won't forget our date for the barbecue tonight."

Pam carried the suitcase loaded with the master disks into the house. She called Stanton Taxi and ordered a cab. Thor got some fresh fruit out of the fridge for a snack.

"You might starve until the feast tonight. Best to have something light now," he advised.

Half an hour later, the taxi dropped Pam off at the campaign headquarters. She took the software straight back to the data storage room.

"All done so soon? Safe and sound?" The man who had earlier given her difficulty helped her unload.

She smiled, told him everything was under control, and began to refile the master disks.

"Where are the duplicates?" he asked.

"Sitting in a jukebox."

"But is that safe enough?" Pam wondered later.

She was finding it difficult to relax in the back seat of the taxi with Thor. Part of the problem was the driver. Every time the man turned a corner, he seemed intent on sliding her and Thor out the door. They hadn't bounced into each other so much since the last time they went dancing.

"I hope they have entertainment."

"Wherever we go there's entertainment," Thor joked. "And most of the time we make it."

The sunset lingered across the countryside. Long shadows stretched themselves into fields of darkness. As the taxi carried the two youngsters further away from Stanton, Pamela lost her sense of direction.

"Can you tell me now where we're going?"

"Patience, Pam. It's a surprise."

"Not another one," she moaned. "Kevin was going out tonight, too. I called Mom but he wouldn't even tell her where. Everybody is into surprises lately!"

The taxi turned off the Farmline Road and onto a circular driveway. Lights at the end illuminated a large mansion.

"Sure do have nice friends," commented the driver.

Thor did not respond. He was too busy holding back his laughter as Pamela went through various stages of reaction. Thor paid the fare and they got out.

"How dare you!" Pam punched his arm.

"I told you it was a surprise."

"If it wasn't such a long way out here, I'd go back in that cab."

"You still have a chance," teased Thor.

"But I'm starving," she admitted. "You've been building me up all day for this, Thor Benson, so I might as well save the mayor's campaign some funds by eating here!"

A large banner was strung across the white columns of the mansion. "ART CRANDLES—TOMORROW'S MAN TODAY," it proclaimed.

"I'll bite my tongue if he speaks to me," she promised. "And if you introduce us, I'll kick you!"

A crowd of partygoers mingled on the patio behind the luxurious mansion. Waiters carried trays of hors d'oeuvres, bartenders served an array of juices and drinks, a side of beef was roasting on a huge barbecue pit.

"One of Crandles's ex-partners," commented Pam.

Her sense of humor worried Thor. If they were overheard, it could make the evening difficult for them. He looked around, but no one seemed to be taking any notice of them.

"I'm only interested in seeing who's here and having some fun," he told the girl. "Let's go pick up a tall drink and ramble. Okay?"

As they walked across the carpeted patio, a distant sound came to them from out of the night sky. As it grew louder, the wind swelled. Suddenly, two searchlights switched on. At the bottom of the property line, a circular pattern of yellow lights appeared, outlining a landing pad.

Everyone gathered to watch. Guided by the twin searchlight beams, a jet helicopter descended onto the landing pad. Thor and Pam recognized it at once as the same blue copter they'd spotted after the mysterious propane explosions!

Paper napkins and loose items flew in the downdraft caused by the rotors. The ground lights dimmed when a rear door opened and a ladder was extended out.

"Ted Smyth," said Thor, identifying the first man to disembark. "The campaign manager."

"And here's the double-digit nerd himself," mumbled Pam.

Art Crandles appeared, waving with both arms and grinning broadly. The mayoralty candidate was so busy waving that he lost his footing on the step. He slipped, but Ted Smyth managed to grab his arm at the last moment.

"Smyth really is his right-hand man," someone joked.

The guests followed the procession up to the house. Thor and Pam, however, remained behind, intrigued by the blue jet helicopter.

"I'm positive that's the same one," they agreed.

To their surprise, another person climbed out of the copter.

"My brother!" blurted Pam.

CHAPTER 9
Strange Operations

"What are you doing here?"

Three voices asked the question at once. Pamela was surprised to see her brother in the helicopter, Kevin wondered why his sister had came to the opposition's party, Thor shared Pam's disbelief.

"Before you say anything else, I checked it already." Kevin indicated the blue copter. "It's a charter craft. The owner rents it by the hour or day only to qualified pilots."

"Then he should know who was flying it that day," Pam concluded.

"If they had used a real name," her brother replied.

Kevin told them the charter pilot's name had been checked and turned out to be false. The identity of his two passengers was also a mystery.

"I'm glad you're here doing something worthwhile with your time, Pammy. Just think, you could be wasting it in Stanton working for Griffin!"

"Eat a peach, Kevin!"

"Splice it!" Thor cut in. "I invited her."

"And who invited you?"

Kevin spun on his heels and walked away from them. His role as Crandles's youth chairman seemed to require his attention again.

"That's the price of his flight ticket," Pam noted bitterly.

They watched Kevin blend into a group of people much older than himself. It became obvious that he was trying hard to impress them. His attitude had changed completely from the moment he left the couple.

Pamela asked if they could leave soon. Thor refused, reminding her of his other reasons for being there. One of them was to enjoy an evening out together.

"Learning to put up with things we don't like is part of the game," added the boy.

He took Pam by the arm, leading her toward the entertainment area. Along the way, they stopped for juice refills. Thor picked out a plate of tasty shrimp to share.

"Hold on, there!" smiled an older youth. "You didn't get your dots today!"

Before they could react, he pinned two flashing microdot buttons onto Pam and Thor. The message blinked "ART CRANDLES—NOW."

"Never!" Pam gritted her teeth.

"Remember where we are," Thor whispered through his smile. "When in Rome, do as the Romans."

"So let's roam."

A cross section of Stanton citizenry was on display: businessmen mingled with each other; local research scientists traded bits of news; campaign workers did their best to relax on this night off. Gossip flowed.

As conversations droned around them, Thor and Pamela began to enjoy themselves. They were very interested in who was present and what was being said, the night air was warm, the music was good, and they liked being together. Times like this were precious. Sitting close to each other in the midst of an adult party, they might as well have been invisible. Nobody paid any attention to the young couple; they were their own best company.

"Look at hotlegs," she chortled.

A dozen couples were dancing on the platform beside the musicians' stage. Kevin was trying to keep in step with an older girl. Every time they shifted, he seemed to lose his balance. The girl kept holding him up.

"That's the 'Crandles Shuffle,'" added Thor, referring to the near-fall on the copter stairs. "When you're ready to trip over yourself, somebody is there for support."

They tapped their feet in time to the beat. After they'd finished the plate of shrimp and emptied their juice glasses, the time seemed right.

"Let's dance!"

They both agreed more practice was needed. But what they lacked in experience, they made up for in energetic moves. The band was playing a string of recent hits. Pam and Thor danced on the edge of the crowd, preferring to keep away from Kevin.

While they danced, Thor let his mind rove. He recalled the scene of vandalism at BenDaCon, references to political dirty tricks, the tampered poster of the mayor, the strange canvassers, the one thousand hamburgers, the parking lot where silver-haired Ted Smyth had met two men, the black box he sped off with....

"Hey, sit down! Please!"

Pamela's words brought him back to the present. She was clutching her foot.

"That's the third time you've stepped on my toes," she complained.

"Sorry, I wasn't concentrating."

"No kidding! You looked like you were a million miles away. What's wrong?"

He shrugged and offered to get more refreshments. Meanwhile, Kevin and the older girl had passed by them on their way into the mansion together. Ted Smyth approached the microphone on the stage. The band took a break while he made his speech.

"Ladies and gentlemen," called the silver-haired man. "Welcome to our modest little gathering." His understatement brought a titter of laughter. "Tonight, we honor the only choice for Stanton's future prosperity, our next mayor, Art Crandles!"

Applause greeted the candidate as he strode to the platform, waving and shaking hands with his supporters along the way.

"It's really a pleasure to see so many of my dearest friends here tonight," he began. "We were out campaigning this evening and if the big chopper hadn't been available, we might *still* be on our way here!"

Ted Smyth led the laughter. Thor and Pam exchanged puzzled looks. Was that really a joke?

"Many of you are concerned with the state of business. I'm concerned with the business of state. As your mayor, I guarantee to cancel local taxes on corporations for two years!"

Not surprisingly, the businessmen cheered. As Crandles continued to speak, he kept looking down at his cupped hands.

"Why does he do that?" whispered Pam. "To check if his hands are clean?"

"Ssshhh!" went a woman nearby.

"...and in the event of our high-tech industries losing out to imports, I will take the case to the federal government!" He made additional promises, enough to please all those present. "And I stand by my words! On election day, when you are sitting by the television holding those cable boxes, enter your code and vote the best man for the job!"

"Look at his hands!" Pam quietly exclaimed.

Before Crandles waved, he slipped bits of paper into his side pocket.

"It all has to be spelled out for him. He has to bring notes, even to his own backyard party."

Though Pam and Thor were not impressed by the man's speech, it seemed that most everyone else was. Art Crandles had the smile of a fashion model, the voice of a radio announcer, the movement of a stage actor, and the eyes of a card dealer.

"Why doesn't he be himself?" wondered Pam as she sat on a bench with Thor.

"Because he's too busy trying to follow instructions. Ted Smyth works him like a puppet."

They watched the man move through the audience. Although these people were guests at his mansion, none seemed to receive any special greeting. The reason had to be his recent arrival in Stanton. He'd moved here only four months ago, bought the mansion, and begun promoting himself as a civic supporter.

"Something isn't right," Thor kept thinking.

"Well, it's the Hamburger Girl!"

Ted Smyth, with a drink in his hand, had approached them from behind.

"Right? On the news? Hamburger handouts?" He grinned at Pamela. "But how does a Griffin worker get to come to this lovely country party?"

"She's my guest," Thor spoke up.

The silver-haired man squinted at him. "Oh, yes. You followed our Kevin in the other day. Correct? Wanted some campaign information? Well, at least you're a supporter. But as for this young lady..."

His words trailed off. Ted Smyth kept glancing toward the

mansion doors. He returned a smile and waved to someone passing by before picking up again with the couple.

"Tell me your names. I like to know everyone at my parties."

"I'm Pamela Powell and this is Thor Benson."

Smyth reacted slowly. "Powell?...No, Kevin's sister?"

The girl nodded boldly.

"And you, I didn't hear your name."

"Thor Benson."

"Benson?...Benson Data Consultants?"

"Yes," Thor replied shortly. He was feeling most uncomfortable now.

"Well, I feel most honored." Smyth seemed to be mocking them. "Our youth chairman's sister works for the opposition. And she's sitting here, side by side with the son of the election day supervisor."

An odd smile creased the man's face. He stepped back to make a theatrical bow toward the couple. "Welcome to the winner's celebration."

"The vote has to happen first," reminded Pam.

"Ah, so it does," laughed Ted Smyth. "But never let a little thing like that get in the way of a victory party!"

When Kevin strolled out of the residence a short while later, he spotted the couple sitting by themselves. He approached them with an invitation.

"You haven't been through the place yet? Then follow me."

"No, thanks. The fresh air is better."

"Pam, let Thor decide for himself. I want him to check out one of these rooms."

Their curiosity was aroused. "What is it, Kev?"

"Central command. Come on."

Pamela remained outside by herself. On principle, she

did not want to follow her brother into Crandles's mansion. Besides, enduring Kevin in their own home was bad enough these days without driving out of town for more of the same.

Kevin led Thor upstairs. On the landing, a security guard sat in a glass booth, surrounded by a number of video surveillance screens. Each monitored a different location in and around the mansion.

"Elmo, this is Thor. My best friend."

"Hi, there," Elmo replied in a deep voice.

"I'd like to show him Mr. Smyth's control room."

"Sorry, Kevin. Off-limits."

"But I promise we won't touch anything. Just a quick look."

The security guard leaned forward. "I couldn't let you in even if I wanted. The room is locked." He moved to the side, punched in the appropriate camera number and the scene came to light. "And it's in use. Sorry, Kevin."

Before the youths could see what was on the screen, Elmo switched it off. He shrugged, then resumed flipping through a photo magazine.

"You can tell me about it anyway," Thor said to his friend on the way downstairs. The surveillance equipment had intrigued him. There was more than enough gear there for safeguarding a rural residence; they must be using it for other purposes as well.

"Wave to Elmo," Kevin smiled.

A tiny camera was spinning in a ceiling mount. It tracked the boys into one of the main rooms. More people had gathered and were partying there. Kevin pointed up to yet another camera watching the area.

"What do they have here?" Thor wondered. He decided to find out.

"Kevin, help me out on this." He whispered his plan.

From the banquet table, Kevin picked out a fine selection of foods. He arranged them all neatly on a plate, put a napkin underneath, and carried the serving upstairs.

Elmo had watched the boy's progress on several video monitors. What surprised the guard was having the food plate set before him.

"That's real kind of you," Elmo told him.

As the man picked at a delicacy, Kevin scanned the bank of screens. On one, he saw Pamela seated outside the patio. She was chatting with the older girl who had danced with him.

"Can you zoom with that?"

Elmo nodded as he ate, pleased that someone was showing an interest in his work. Besides, he liked Kevin. At a meeting early in the campaign, the youth chairman had been introduced to the staff and had impressed them all.

"Sure, there we go," Elmo said between bites.

The camera image moved in for close-ups on different people on the patio. One screen suddenly went dark.

"Not again," he murmured. "Gotta fix that mounting. Can you stand by here just in case?"

Of course, the boy agreed.

No sooner had the guard walked down the stairs than Thor stode out from a nearby doorway. His plan had worked, but he had only a short time to act.

"Let me take his seat." Thor shifted in behind the glass booth. "Which room is it?"

Kevin pressed a button on the control panel. The image on video screen #8 faded in. Thor reached for a small pair of earphones and plugged them in under the picture tube.

They saw two men bent over a black box in the room. Surrounding them was a glittering display of high-tech equipment.

"That stuff is all state-of-the-art!" exclaimed Thor. He had seen some of it featured on science programs. "None of it is available yet!"

"Then how do they have it?"

As the two men continued working on the black box, Kevin pressed the camera zoom to magnify the image. A close-up of the box filled the screen. In gold lettering, they saw its identification: "C.A.S.E. 4."

The men's words filtered through the earphones. "...another test connection...reset the band-pass filters ...At-Home Shopping scanner..."

Kevin reversed the camera zoom, showing the men in detail. Thor remembered their faces from the Binary Avenue parking lot. They were the ones who had given Ted Smyth the black box!

"...use the same intercept signal....key the referendum votes.... redirect the P.A.C...." Thor suddenly realized what the men were planning.

"They're going to sabotage the electronic voting results!"

He slipped the earphones off and placed them on the desk. Kevin had noticed his friend's startled reaction and switched off the monitor. Neither youth had noticed a door open down the hall. A shadow loomed behind them.

"So the MicroKidz are at work again?" hissed a menacing voice.

Art Crandles had been watching!

CHAPTER 10
A Case of the Mistaken C.A.S.E.

Elmo the security guard had found nothing wrong with the surveillance camera. The problem was a paper napkin that somebody had taped over the camera lens.

"Who'd do a thing like that?" Elmo muttered as he tore the napkin loose.

When he reached the stairway, the answer became obvious. Elmo saw Thor Benson and Kevin Powell seated in his glass booth. The owner of the mansion, Art Crandles, was questioning the pair.

"Never mind," Crandles said as Elmo tried to explain. "I want to hear it from them."

"I'll get Mr. Smyth," offered the guard.

The boys claimed they had been watching only the monitors that were on. Fortunately, Thor had disconnected the earphone from output #8 when Kevin switched it off. No evidence of their secret viewing remained.

"I had the feeling you'd be up here sooner or later," Smyth growled.

"Very sorry for leaving my post, sir, but a camera was not..."

"Yes, Elmo," interrupted Smyth, as he continued glaring

at the boys. "Is there any need for you two to be up here? No? Then let's move it."

Another door in the hallway opened. Two men walked out of the high-tech equipment room, acknowledged Crandles and Smyth, then continued to a rear exit.

"Hurry up," Smyth prodded the youths.

They were being ejected from the party. The worst part for Kevin was missing the side of beef on the barbecue. He would have to do with a quick snack at the Byte.

"Oh, Pam!" called Thor.

She was still talking to the older girl. Kevin walked out onto the patio to speak to her. Pamela rose and followed him to the door.

"We have to leave so soon?"

"A taxi happens to be on its way, especially for you three," replied Ted Smyth.

"But who ordered it?"

"I did," smiled the silver-haired man. "We've had complaints about children here."

He looked directly at Thor and Kevin as he spoke.

"Taxi's waiting, Mr. Smyth."

Elmo escorted Thor and Pamela directly to the cab. Smyth had a final exchange with Kevin in the front room.

"What did he say?" they asked when he got into the taxi.

Kevin put a finger to his lips. He preferred not to discuss the situation in the cab. He wasn't certain that this taxi driver was not another Smyth employee. They returned to Stanton in silence.

"That's okay," the driver told them. "Already paid for."

Thor awoke, as always, shortly after dawn. The sunlight, which he used as a kind of natural alarm clock, trickled through his open window. He crept into the kitchen for a quiet breakfast. While his parents slept soundly, the boy began to organize his day. He checked the RND micro for messages and found only three inquiries awaiting his father.

Out in the workshop, Thor began Mr. Chips's daily cleaning routine. Even though the robot's heat-resistant, anti-magnetic torso contained a wealth of stacked data disks, a simple press on a button accomplished menial tasks as well.

"Get that floor shining," said the boy as he watched the robot extend its vacuum hose.

Then he settled down to more serious matters. The CREX+ microcomputer fed back the previous day's report. Thor found what he wanted under the TeleMail listings.

"TWENTY-FOUR COMMUNIQUÉS BETWEEN THE CRANDLES MANSION AND HIS CAMPAIGN OFFICES," the boy read aloud from the display monitor, "AND A 318 BYPASS TO ONE CORPORATE LINE."

This indicated a special call from the mansion to an unknown building in Stanton. The time of the call caught the boy's attention.

"Let's check the final shutdown at BenDaCon," he thought.

Since the CREX+ had a remote link into the former BenDaCon mainframe computer, it provided a timed record of incoming data.

"Our office went off-line at 3:18 A.M. Just before the vandals broke in."

The identical times made his deduction simple. The BenDaCon system crashed precisely at the time a private transfer came from the Crandles mansion. His father's security and surveillance programs then became a very easy target.

Should he awaken his father? Thor decided against it. Edward Benson needed all the sleep he could get.

For the next three hours, Thor worked on developing a new computer program. He called it the "*Data Snatcher Trap*." When it was done, he ran it through the CREX+ for a final verification.

"Ready for some food, Chips?"

He secured the cable link between the robot and the micro disk drives and inserted the new floppy diskette platter inside his micro-age jukebox.

Laraine Benson came over to the workshop later that morning.

"How long have you been out here?"

Thor told her and asked if his father was awake yet.

"He left an hour ago."

"Where was he going?"

"Not to the office, that's for certain," she confided. "They won't be able to supervise the election procedures from there. The damage was too extensive. He went somewhere for a meeting about changing the voting plans."

Thor followed his mother back into the house. Because of her schedule at the Flexercise Center, Mrs. Benson wanted to complete her grocery shopping early. She sat down in front of the fibre-optic relayer and picked up the ordering panel.

"What's wrong with the At-Home Shopping?" she called out a moment later. "The whole system is down."

Thor tried it. None of the stores listed reacted to the PURCHASE REQUEST button.

"I'll plug in a test on the CREX+," he said, leaving the room.

Before he had even reached the workshop, his mother called out. Apparently, the service had returned to normal.

"Why should it function one moment and not the next?" he wondered.

No sooner had the question formed in his mind, than he

recalled last evening's conversation. ". . . . reset the bandpass filters. . . At-Home Shopping scanner. . . "

It was those two men in the mansion operating the black box C.A.S.E.! Thor realized he had been the only one wearing earphones, and the only one who overheard their plans. No one else, not even Kevin, knew the threatening potential of the black box!

Meanwhile, Kevin had returned to Crandles's campaign headquarters that morning. It was business as usual for him. He still had numerous duties to fulfill. Sure, there had been that embarrassing departure from the mansion last night, but was it really his fault?

"Thor was the one who taped the napkin to the camera," he reasoned.

When he got to his desk, he found Ted Smyth waiting for him.

"Your connections go a lot deeper than I'd suspected," the silver-haired man began. "Your sister campaigns for the mayor, your best friend works with his father who happens to be supervising the voting, and you help control our data analysis. Very cosy. The MicroKidz have all the bases covered, don't they?"

"It's not like you think."

"Then what were you doing upstairs last night during the party? All the other guests were downstairs enjoying themselves. Why weren't you?"

"You took me into that communications room last week," Kevin said nervously. "You seemed real proud of it. I found it fascinating. I told you that, right? But Elmo wouldn't let me show it to Thor, who I knew wanted to see it. That's all! We didn't get in! And when you asked us to leave, we did. But look, I'm here this morning, back to help as usual."

Ted Smyth rolled his eyes. Since he'd dug up more

information about the MicroKidz that morning, his suspicions had surged. But the last thing he needed prior to the election was a disturbance.

The campaign smile returned. "Fine, but on one condition. You stay on as youth chairman, but data processing is no longer your assignment."

Kevin shrugged. "You're the boss."

"We can use your ability elsewhere," the man grinned. "For instance, there's the breakfast on election day morning at the Stanton Senior Citizens' Home."

The job did not enthrall the youth. He preferred a more technical role, but felt he had no choice at this point.

"You're a smart lad," Smyth said in parting. "We have plans for you."

"Mr. Hines?"
"Who's that? Oh, Thor."
"Can I speak with you?"
"Certainly. Go ahead."
"Not over the VistaPhone, sir."
"I understand. Come right over."

There had been too many interceptions already. Thor was not sure which data transmission line to trust. The only safe form of conversation was face to face.

He arrived at the federal building within the hour. Hines and two associates were waiting for him.

"So, something has broken since our last discussion?"

Thor cleared his throat.

"Those smugglers? Of the high-tech gear?"
"Yes, Thor, go on."
"I think I know who they are."

The investigators leaned forward intently. This was obviously the good news they had hoped for. However, they were not prepared for his accusations.

"This is very serious," Hines said, when they'd heard the names.

"That's why I didn't want to say it over the VistaPhone. They have an interceptor that can listen in or change anything they want. I saw it."

"Were there markings on it?" asked one of the men.

"Only the word 'CASE.'"

"C.A.S.E.?"

"Yes, that's what I meant. What does it stand for?"

Mr. Hines wrote it out. "COMPUTER AUTHORIZED SYSTEMS EXCHANGER."

"Which ties in exactly with data interceptions and alterations" added his associate.

Thor kept silent while the men considered their next move. He heard that C.A.S.E. was a restricted telecommunications device. It was privately manufactured in Switzerland by a firm that produced only four models a year. Each was sold under strict license to control their use. Obtaining a unit required millions of dollars and special clearance. The penalty for importing a C.A.S.E. without government permission was ten years in prison.

"We need more evidence to get a warrant," Hines said.

Thor offered a suggestion. "What about the helicopter?"

"The first one you kids saw that day?" asked Hines.

"It's a charter craft. I saw it last night. Guess who was in it."

Hines guessed correctly.

Edward Benson waited for his son in their backyard workshop. He was the only adult who knew the code to the digital deadbolt lock.

"Who told you about the C.A.S.E.?" Thor asked, when his father confronted him.

"Sergeant Dalby. Hines obtained his warrants there," the man said slowly. "I hope you are absolutely certain, Thor. This is very serious."

"Honest, Dad. It's all out there."

To further convince him, Thor gave him the printout sheets showing the times of the data transfers. He circled the final message input received by the BenDaCon mainframe. With another circle, he identified the exact time of the transmission output from the Crandles mansion.

"Doesn't that prove they logged on and overrode the surveillance program?" concluded the boy.

Edward shook his head. "It may be coincidence."

"Then what about the C.A.S.E.?"

Mr. Benson knew about Computer Authorized Systems Exchangers. Their potential for industrial and military applications had been profiled in recent technical conferences.

"I just didn't think one would come into the country this fast," he admitted. "And worse, to be used against us!"

He spoke, not as a private businessman, but as a corporate citizen. The presence of this C.A.S.E., if indeed it was in Stanton, greatly affected the upcoming election.

"What will happen?"

"We're in a real mess. Our security for the fibre-optic voting process is gone. Those vandals destroyed that software, master copies included," he said in disgust. Then, after a moment of reflection, Mr. Benson declared, "The whole nation is watching us because the next federal election will have electronic balloting. That C.A.S.E. has to be seized!"

Two vans parked outside 208 Matrix Boulevard.

"They're here," Thor said, looking through the curtains.

"Please be careful," Laraine urged.

Edward pulled on a dark jacket. He kissed his wife and started out the door. Thor did likewise and followed.

Plainclothes detectives waited in the vans. Thor and his father climbed into the second vehicle. The sun was just setting as they sped off. Sergeant Dalby was seated across from the Bensons. He gave the boy a bemused expression, as if he doubted his wild story. Everyone else considered it deadly serious. Mr. Hines sat up front beside the driver.

There was no conversation over the cellular radios because they were easily monitored. The operation had to be a complete surprise.

"Here's the plan," a detective said, passing around an instruction sheet. "Any questions?"

There were none. The responsibility for action now rested with the team of special officers in the front van.

As they drew close to the Crandles mansion, the lead vehicle continued up the driveway. Its passengers had the weapons and warrants. It was their duty to seize the building quickly.

The second van blocked the entrance to the driveway. Everyone waited for the signal. The tension level rose with each passing second. Sweat broke out on the Bensons' foreheads. To the other officers, this was simply another raid. To Thor and Edward, it was torture.

Blip. Blip. The alert sounded!

"Here we go!" shouted a detective.

The van tore ahead, the passengers lurching against their seatbelts. Seconds later, the vehicle screeched to a halt in front of the mansion.

"Stay close behind," Sergeant Dalby advised.

His weapon was drawn. Mr. Hines, Thor, and his father followed the officers. The excitement of the raid infected the boy. He was overjoyed to know that the C.A.S.E. would be seized, the vandals arrested, and election security restored.

The senior detective in charge came rushing downstairs. He cast an enraged look at the youth. "You! Upstairs!"

Edward Benson reacted defensively. "What's that?"

"Trouble! Big trouble!" the detective yelled back.

Two other detectives from the first van ran downstairs and brushed past them.

"Get up here!" screamed another. "Bring that kid who sent us!"

Thor and his father climbed the staircase.

"Secret high-tech gear, huh?" smirked the lead detective.

He swung open the door. The Bensons peered inside and saw a room filled with blinking video games. All the secret computer equipment had been removed!

CHAPTER 11
ZAPPED!

"Do you think we fooled them?"

"For now. We only need two days."

"That's all I want!" bellowed Art Crandles.

"The election is ours!" agreed Ted Smyth.

They had moved into a modest rural homestead, ten miles from the mansion. That property had become too hot. From this new base, they would direct the Crandles-for-Mayor campaign, right through to a vote-tampered victory.

"We simply broadcast the rest of our video commercials, you speak at the senior citizens' breakfast tomorrow morning, and that evening..." Ted Smyth began to convulse in anticipation of the win.

Art Crandles loved the forecast. The cue cards for his victory speech were already prepared.

"Don't you think this is much neater? Having a victory celebration before the election!" roared Art.

"That's the system in some countries."

"What is?"

"They announce the results—before the voting!"

They toasted their assured win with champagne. An ice

bucket and bottle sat on the black box in the center of the room. It was the C.A.S.E. 4.

"I rest my case," laughed Smyth.

He filled the glasses again. "A toast! Our continued success! All the way to the nation's capitol!"

A political revolution was underway.

"All those video games, Art. That was a stroke of genius!"

"If the police want to listen to a kid, it's their own fault," snorted Crandles as he gulped the champagne. "We didn't invite them."

Smyth patted the side of the C.A.S.E.

"A good thing we overheard them."

A moving van was parked in front of the Bensons' garage. Burly men were loading it with Thor's computer equipment. His workshop was being dismantled. One of the movers was carrying out Mr. Chips.

"No! Leave him!" shouted the boy.

The men had been ordered to clear the laboratory, but they replaced the robot when Mr. Benson spoke to them. Coming so soon after the failed police raid on the Crandles mansion, this movement seemed like a punishment to Thor.

Edward Benson spoke to his son.

"I hope you understand. It's only for a short time."

The youth nodded, staring at the ground.

"I believe that what you saw in that room was the C.A.S.E. Smyth must have had advance warning, moved all the smuggled gear, then set us up to look foolish."

"It sure worked," muttered the youth. "Everyone else thinks I'm a liar."

Edward tried to ease Thor's misery. "Loaning this equipment might help change their attitude. Think about it. My office was destroyed. Where were the detectives who were supposed to be protecting it? Our only chance now for supervising the election is to use the CREX+, the rest of your lab gear, and whatever we can borrow in town."

Put that way, Thor felt better. After all, that the police raid failed was not his fault; they should have been more careful about discussing it over VistaPhones and TeleMail. The mistakes that had been allowed to occur must now be corrected.

He waved goodbye as his father joined the men in the moving truck. The CREX+ and related gear were to be set up in the BenDaCon offices. Hopefully, two things would be restored: security for the election and Thor's confidence.

"Lots of action going on," observed Pam, strolling up the driveway.

"Woke you up?"

"Only when I saw them carting out most of the workshop."

"Dad needs some backup in the office."

"Yeah?" She seemed puzzled. "Say, where were you last night?"

Thor had been told that the faulty raid was to be kept secret. "Oh, just out and about," he shrugged.

Pam didn't challenge him. She knew that when Thor didn't want to talk, there was no point in pushing him.

"Mayor Griffin is planning a big rally tonight," she reminded him. "Election eve party. Want to be my guest?"

"I had my fill of political parties the other night. No thanks."

She persisted. "This will be different. More informal. Lots of young people for a change."

Again, he declined. They began to discuss Kevin's continuing work for the Crandles campaign. Apparently, the ejection from the barbecue hadn't affected him.

"What does?" wondered Thor.

"You get a chance to ask him now."

They saw Kevin come out of the Powell house. He got into his car, started it up, and drove across the road. He stopped on Thor's driveway, right beside the couple.

"He's giving me a lift into town," she winked while getting into the passenger seat. "Isn't that kind?"

Thor leaned over. "How is nice Mr. Smyth?"

"Who cares?"

"Everything okay at headquarters?" he prodded.

"No, everything is not okay!" came the angry reply. Thor had touched a nerve. "I help plan a street canvas and nobody clears it! My data collection files are frozen! I'm the youth chairman but have nothing to do!"

"So why are you still there?"

Kevin sneered. "'Cause I want to be with a winner!"

The wheels on the sports car burned into the pavement. The Powells sped off, leaving behind an isolated friend.

"One at a time, please!"

More people were trying to squeeze through the door. BenDaCon's reception area was already overcrowded. The staff had to hold people back from barging into the conference room.

"Next! Gift Boutique!" yelled an employee above the noise.

The store's manager forced his way through the crush. He was led into the conference room where Edward Benson and three associates were sitting. The manager's story was a familiar one.

"I'm holding your firm responsible for all financial losses!" he shouted. "You're supposed to provide security on the At-Home Shopping service! You failed! My business is near collapse! Somebody has transferred all the money through my banking code!"

"Please, if you will listen..." was all Edward managed to say before he was interrupted.

"This video shopping idea is crazy!"

Another staff member took the manager by the arm. "Our policy will cover your loss, sir. You can give me the details out here."

He was maneuvered into another room, and quiet was momentarily restored. Edward looked at his associates. They were all glum at the prospect of facing more angry clients.

"Take their claims outside and we'll be in touch," he directed an aide.

The furious shop owners were already waiting when he had arrived that morning. Their complaints were all the same. The electronic At-Home Shopping and Banking service had left them on the edge of bankruptcy.

"We have some important decisions to make," continued Edward Benson.

They discussed the security for election day. Since the same two-way fibre-optic system that carried those other services was to be used to register the votes, a major threat loomed.

"I'll consider the alternatives," Mr. Benson concluded at the end of the meeting. "How is our backup assembly going?"

"A few more hours, sir. Some of it's giving us trouble because there seems to be no set pattern," reported an aide. "We won't have the same computing power, but a control center will be ready."

Two hours later, Thor arrived.

"So you did get the message," Edward said, relieved.

"Mrs. Powell came over and told me. What's up?"

The man took his son aside. "I don't want to embarrass them," Edward told Thor, indicating a group of technicians working nearby. "But they don't have a clue about reassembling your lab setup. Would you mind?"

The boy was only too happy to assist. "Why didn't you ask me in at the beginning?"

The reason involved security matters, part of the aftermath of the raid, Edward explained.

Assured of no interruptions, Thor proceeded to take over the job. He found all the other equipment installed and functioning. Only the CREX+ and two phase limiters remained offline.

"And the *Data Snatcher Trap!*" he exclaimed quietly.

Thor's most recent computer program was still at home. He would have to return and pick it up before the voting began. As an implanted memory circuit blown into the CREX+, the *Data Snatcher Trap* was a super-secure PROM. This Programmable Read-Only Memory stored a fixture to prevent the C.A.S.E. from breaking through.

"At least that's my theory," he said to himself. He dared not mention this new development until he could test it. "And to do that, I'll have to wait for Crandles and Smyth to use the C.A.S.E."

Thor was sure they would. The election was tomorrow.

"All done?" Edward asked in surprise.

"An hour is lots of time," Thor replied.

Everyone at the mayor's reelection headquarters was involved in the plans for the evening rally. Entertainment, refreshments, balloons, microdot buttons, and fireworks were scheduled. This would be Mayor Gwen Griffin's last chance for a get-together with her supporters.

"I want to leave a personal message for all our supporters and the undecided voters," she stated.

"A great idea, but how can that be done?" asked one worker.

The mayor pointed to the back rooms. "Our data files!"

A computer would insert each name in a standard letter, then beam it directly into the voter's home on the TeleMail line!

"We can send five thousand messages an hour," reported Pamela. She had been called out of the data storage area, along with the older man in charge.

"And I'll add a special memo to each home," mused Gwen Griffin. "Something like, 'Participating in our nation's first electronic election proves that the future is already here. Continue this advance forward with the administration that helped bring it to you.' How's that?"

"A bit windy, but I'll work on it," said the older man.

The mayor was pleased at the activity. Volunteers came in off the street to help load the supply vehicles. Everyone agreed that the rally would be the campaign highlight.

To say that the atmosphere in the Crandles headquarters was subdued, would be putting it mildly. The mood was slack, the campaign workers not motivated.

"Seems like they don't want anybody's suggestions," several young volunteers complained.

"We might as well be machines," said another. "Unplugged when they don't need us."

Ted Smyth contributed to their negative attitudes. The silver-haired man had become withdrawn. He no longer stopped to chat on his way through the building but simply went directly to his office and closed the door. The volunteers were puzzled by this change in him.

"I've put so much into this, I don't want to quit," admitted Kevin to several co-workers.

They agreed. Besides, they believed their candidate had a winning edge.

Meanwhile, the office data analyst had made a startling discovery. At first he thought the problem was electrical. He conducted more tests; the results proved negative. Finally, he staggered out of the computer room.

"We've lost it all!" he gasped.

Kevin hurried from his desk to prevent the man from falling. Everyone came over and surrounded them.

"We lost what?" Kevin asked.

"Our programs, supporters lists, membership files, all our financial records!" shrieked the man. "But it's not my fault! I swear it!"

His cry pierced the air. Hours of overwork, staring at tiny figures on cathode ray tubes, had broken him.

Ted Smyth opened his office door. "Quiet out there!"

"You'd better come out, sir," advised Kevin.

"For what? I'm having a vidiconference!"

Kevin explained the dire situation.

"So, that's what happens!" barked Smyth.

He closed his office door on them. The campaign manager seemed not to care about restoring the system.

"We're down," reported Pamela.

"How's that? We just started the output!"

The older man saw the blank loading signals. "You're right! We're zapped! All our data is erased!"

They notified Mayor Griffin at once. The extent of the problem became evident. Her individual notices would never reach the people, and the undecided voters would be ignored at this crucial time.

"And our Election Eve Rally might be cancelled!"

Since that was also programmed into their databank, the event was in danger of falling through. Coordination of the entertainers, crowd control, assembly times, parking assistance, refreshment orders—even the fireworks display—everything stored in the computer's memory bank had disappeared!

By this time, they had heard about the similar catastrophe at Crandles's headquarters. That, however, did not solve their problems.

Gwen Griffin nervously paced the office. "Isn't there any method to pull it all back?"

Pamela surprised everyone with her outburst.

"The jukebox principle!"

CHAPTER 12
E-Day

"Election day! And the electronic eyes of the nation are upon Stanton!"

The Satellite News Network led the broadcast of events leading to this historic day. Announcers, media analysts, and federal politicians spoke on the effect this would have for the whole country.

"The electronic election will bring fundamental changes to democracy! Today we enter a new era!"

Art Crandles and Ted Smyth, seated in the rear of their white limousine, were also watching the reports. Mounted in a console, the TV screen was surrounded by a miniaturized computer facility. A printer, disk drives, cellular radiophone, VistaPhone, and portable keyboard completed the limo's rich furnishings.

A Stanton reporter was reviewing last evening's events. ". . . . but still the mayor's rally went on as planned. It was a great success, with thousands of her supporters attending. For a while, though, the occasion was in jeopardy. A sudden breakdown in the data system nearly prevented the final details and invitations from going out . . . ."

"Too bad they did," muttered Crandles.

"So how did she do it?" wondered Smyth.

"...until the arrival of this creature," continued the reporter. The televised picture showed Mr. Chips plugged by cable into a VistaPhone. "....Stanton's young inventor, Thor Benson, let his personal robot come to the rescue! Would you describe what happened next?"

Pamela Powell appeared on the screen. "I copied all our disks with Thor, and for safekeeping, stored them inside here," she said opening the front panel of the robot. She demonstrated how the jukebox assembly went into action by shifting several floppy diskettes. "Mr. Chips bypassed the troubled TeleMail system and plugged directly into the VistaPhone. He wasn't as fast as the other method, but he managed two thousand calls per hour."

"*Only* two thousand an hour?" exclaimed the interviewer. "That's more calls than I could make in a year!"

"Blast!" shouted Crandles as he shut off the television.

The men contemplated their next move. With Elmo acting as chauffeur, they were racing toward a showdown.

"We change none of our plans," Smyth decided. "So what if they have a robot that spews out mailing lists? Remember, Art, the boys did a real good job on BenDaCon. I bet they're still having trouble just getting the lights to work!"

The mayoralty candidate smiled. "Sure. Those voting supervisors are probably using hand calculators. No competition for our C.A.S.E.!"

"Congratulations, Mister Mayor!"

They both laughed.

An Election Day breakfast had been arranged at the Stanton Senior Citizens' Home. It was to be a low-key affair; Art Crandles would meet the elderly voters and chat over coffee and donuts. One local cablecaster stood by with his camera crew.

"The old and the new," whispered Ted Smyth into the man's ear. "Many of these old folks were born before TV was invented. Now they're shaking hands with a person about to be elected through a fibre-optics ballot!"

Again Smyth proved his skill as a campaign manager. The announcer repeated Smyth's words when the report was aired. Art Crandles glowed on the screen as he waved and smiled and made his way through the elderly group.

"Campaign television at its best," whistled Smyth.

Several volunteers were present to assist at the event. Kevin Powell managed the arrangements as ordered. He handed out microdot buttons wherever the camera pointed.

"I happened to see your sister on the news," Ted Smyth told him later. "That robot is quite an invention."

"Oh, yeah. Thor's toy. He develops something new every second day."

Smyth decided that Thor knew too much. He might still upset their plans.

"If I can't keep tabs on that one, I'll take the nearest I can get," the silver-haired man decided.

As soon as Crandles had concluded the meeting with handshakes, everyone returned to the white limousine. Smyth called Kevin over.

"Why don't you come along and watch the election results with us?"

"This is it!"

E-Day had arrived! Months of planning were now focused on these few hours. The BenDaCon staff had their alternate system in operation. What the vandals had tried to disrupt, the staff had restored.

"We're not functioning at the expected capacity, but these backups will see us through the day," Edward Benson told his employees.

After the pep talk, the applications specialists went to their positions. They seated themselves on the folding chairs brought in to replace the cushioned swirlers sent out for repairs. The display monitors carrying data were on loan from a nearby video shop. All the computers, modems, and drives had been gathered from private homes and stores.

Thor paced in the background, leaving the programmers and analysts to their jobs. His only duty was to assist in repairing or reconnecting the hardware taken from his workshop lab.

"POLLS OPEN IN ONE HOUR," flashed a notice.

This indicated the time when the At-Home Shopping and Banking service lines would undergo a transfer. Instead of the televised products and figures displayed in each residence, referendum questions and a choice of candidates for town council would appear. The slate for mayor was scheduled at the end of the programming.

"Let's run those refs again," shouted one man.

A programmer on the other side of the large office punched in the "REFERENDUM" ballot. Twenty questions came up on the screen.

"Test Propositions #8 and #17," came the order.

These questions concerned the Change in Land Use Bylaw and the Increase in Day Care Services. The programmer entered in test codes on behalf of fifty voters. Choices were made, either "YES" or "NO." He entered the selections, fed the data through, and awaited the results.

Seconds later came his victorious yell, "All systems are go!"

There was no turning back. The future had arrived in Stanton.

Thor anticipated, that if there was going to be trouble, it would be soon. He stepped up to the CREX+ and opened the rear microcircuitry gate.

"What are you doing there, Thor?"

"Securing a PROM program, Dad."

Mr. Benson wanted to know exactly what he was doing.

"It's my *Data Snatcher Trap*. To neutralize the C.A.S.E.," he said quietly, as they walked into a smaller office.

"But how can that happen?"

"By comparing changes in the direct electronic output to each residence with the returning input. The difference should indicate when the C.A.S.E. is in use," replied the boy. "And it should tell us where the device is!"

"Even trace its location?"

The security of the election process suddenly seemed assured. It was the best moment Edward Benson had had all week.

"Visitor in the lobby," reported a secretary.

"Sorry, no one is allowed in."

"But he insists," said the voice on the intercom. "It's a Mr. Hines."

The aviation investigator was led through to the office. Thor guessed that a break had occurred and he was right. Hines lifted a mini-cassette player from his pocket.

"A follow-up that I know you will find useful," he explained. "After Thor's claim that he saw a C.A.S.E., and the police raid, we reviewed all the information relating to that initial, bizarre incident." He was referring, of course, to the abandoned plane left near the barn which was destroyed by the propane explosions.

Mr. Benson looked at his son. He wondered what this had to do with the present events. Hines inserted a tape cassette into the player.

"This is the recording received by the Stanton control tower prior to the landing," he said as the machine started.

". . . . Reserve power is negative! Come get us! Case secure! Repeat, case secure! We're going in!"

Hines stopped the tape. He reversed it to play the last phrases.

"...Case secure! Repeat, case secure!"

"I'm positive that's the Computer Authorized Systems Exchanger he's referring to," declared the aviation investigator, "letting the ground crew know the smuggled material was safe."

"I see what you mean," replied Edward.

"And we also realize the implications of that C.A.S.E. being used," added Mr. Hines.

A shout came from the staff outside the small office.

"Election data coming online!"

The black box rested on the living room floor. Beside it sat the high-tech apparatus that threatened free elections. The C.A.S.E. resembled an old microwave oven that had been opened up and customized with an assortment of buttons, digital meters, nanosecond time coders, and energy analyzers. A transceiver formed the main control function. Under a built-in keyboard were four tiny video display monitors whose amber screens lit up the rest of the device.

"Looks almost harmless," commented Art Crandles.

"Until we start it," Ted Smyth reminded him.

They were joined by the two specialists who programmed the C.A.S.E.; they were also its smugglers.

"Where's the boy?" asked one.

"Outside," Elmo replied from the next room. "Walking around."

"Good. Keep him away from this."

"He won't be a problem," said the silver-haired man.

A color television set in the corner of the room carried the Referendum listings. Two men waited for instructions.

"Wait for Propositions #14 to #18," Smyth told them. "When they come up, I'd like to see them win by a 10 to 15 percent margin. But vary each one. We don't want to arouse any suspicions."

The men spliced the fibre-optic cable into the C.A.S.E. Now they could control the outcome of every vote.

"Explain it to me again," Crandles asked. "I want to know exactly how this thing works. After all, this is my day!"

"Every voter is registered with a Personal Authorization Code," one of the specialists began. "We pulled those out from the At-Home Shopping and Banking service lines."

"We did that with the first C.A.S.E., but it gave us problems. It messed up the TeleMail and shopping ports too easily, so that's why this second, newer unit had to be delivered. Saving the best for last."

His partner continued. "Now, when a voter presses his P.A.C. number at home, a computer at BenDaCon opens a space for him to register his vote. It relays back a 'READY' signal.

"Which is when the C.A.S.E. cuts in! It signals the authorized code return but exchanges this system," he tapped the digital meters, "for the one which the person at home uses. No matter what they press, it still registers whatever we order."

"You can make us win by a landslide or a squeaker?"

They nodded in unison. "We're correct to within .0024 percent of the ballot."

Crandles and Smyth quietly considered their entry into federal politics.

Kevin Powell continued to wander the grounds.
"Not a bad place for the summer," he thought.

After fiddling with the communications console in the rear of the limousine, he became restless. He could have gone into the house, but the expressions of those two other men unnerved him. What else was there to do?

"What about the barn?" he wondered.

The structure was in need of repairs. Located a hundred feet from the reconditioned homestead, the barn had obviously been neglected for years. It looked so hazardous from the outside that Kevin couldn't imagine that anyone would want to get in.

"Then why put those big new locks on it?" he asked himself.

Curiosity took hold. With a bit of pressure, he was able to kick in two loose boards to make an opening wide enough to squeeze through.

He found bales of hay and old farm tools strewn about inside. A canvas sheet caught the boy's attention. It covered two huge wooden crates, the sort used for shipping.

"Wonder what they're storing," he said to himself.

He pulled off the canvas cover. Foreign words were stamped on the crates. Kevin didn't know the language, but he wanted to know what it identified. He raised the lid of one of the crates.

"Oh, boy!" he whistled.

A shining collection of high-tech equipment lay beneath him. Kevin realized this must be the smuggler's load.

Fast checks of the other crates convinced him. Medical, research, industrial, and military hardware filled the containers awaiting shipment. He didn't know where it was all going, but he did know that Mr. Hines should be notified.

"In the limo! There's a cellular radio!" he remembered.

He folded down the canvas flaps and checked to ensure that nothing had been disturbed. Then he returned to the crack in the barn siding and squeezed through.

Kevin's last thought before striking the ground was, "Who did that?"

A broken barn board was tossed beside his crumpled body.

"Anything happen yet?"

"Everything seems to be normal."

"How about on your side?"

"Just tell me what normal means these days."

BenDaCon technicians were monitoring the incoming votes. From one side of the office to the other, the staff called out their comments. The feared attack on the ballot programming had not been detected.

"Maybe they got scared," said Thor.

"Or they're waiting," suggested Edward.

He was surveying the activity on the three video screens in his office. Thor was sitting with him, finishing the last of a lunch platter.

"Who knows? We might be lucky!"

The door opened and two associates entered.

"The Referendum slate is just over and we're going to start the town council selection next," they reported. "But could you check on this first?"

They gathered around the CREX+. A pattern spelling "D.S.T." blinked in one corner of the display monitor.

"We've got it!" Thor shouted excitedly. "That's my program responder, the *Data Snatcher Trap!*"

"But it's only showing on Propositions #14 to #18," his father pointed out.

"Maybe that's all they've used the C.A.S.E. for so far!"

While the adults stood by, the youngster went into action. Since this strange program had been entered without their knowledge, they could only watch in fascination. Edward Benson, however, was aware of the strategy.

"Steady... steady... holding... there!"

The boy gave a sigh of relief when the CREX + memory storage had completed tracing the input. Thor Benson pointed proudly to the address that appeared on the screen.

"The C.A.S.E. transmissions are coming from there!"

"The jet copter's here!" shouted Elmo.

"Hurry up!" yelled Ted Smyth above the clatter of the approaching aircraft.

"I've still got another box," Art Crandles called from the back door.

"We don't have room!" shouted Smyth. "This will take up all the space!"

He indicated the two huge crates stacked nearby. The canvas tops had been pulled off. Identity stickers showed their destinations; each was bound for a hostile foreign country.

"What about him?" Elmo asked.

Kevin Powell lay semiconscious on the canvas pile. A trickle of blood on his head marked where he had been struck.

"We take him along," Smyth said flatly. "Hostages are solid currency."

At the sight of an advancing blue helicopter, the departure activity became more frenzied. The two specialists prepared to move the contraband into their craft before the passengers boarded. With no care for the boy's condition, Elmo tried to shake the youth awake. Kevin's eyes rolled, his knees buckled.

A whirlwind rose around the homestead as the blue helicopter's descent stirred up the dust. The men were forced to cover their eyes.

That was the plan.

"Keep your hands up!"

Six gun-wielding detectives jumped out of the helicopter. They ran to each of the men and forced them to the ground. As the rotors slowed, Sergeant Dalby, Mr. Hines, Thor, and Edward Benson leaped from the cargo door.

Kevin Powell stirred when he heard their voices. He opened his eyes when Mr. Benson tapped his head.

"Guess what?" Kevin said faintly.

"What?" asked Thor.

"I know who didn't win."

Thor smiled at his friend and helped Mr. Benson carry the boy to the copter.

The detectives, meanwhile, had locked handcuffs on the five criminals. Thor glared at them all, saving his fiercest looks for Ted Smyth and Art Crandles.

"You won something you both deserve," spat the youth. "Ten years!"

Sergeant Dalby and Mr. Hines raised the top of one of the shipping crates to examine the smuggled high-tech hardware.

"Ten years?" roared the policeman. "Try ten times ten years!"

CHAPTER 13

Final Recount

Election results were released seconds after the computer poll closed. The predicted landslide win occurred, but not in the way Art Crandles and Ted Smyth had planned.

"MAYOR GWEN GRIFFIN REELECTED!" flashed the notice.

By an overwhelming margin, the people of Stanton had given their support to the person whose success in the past assured them of a brighter future. Many showed up for the celebration at her headquarters.

"An honest victory," Pamela said when she saw Thor. "We won for all the right reasons."

He agreed wholeheartedly. His part in making this first electronic election free from corruption became news later that evening.

Kevin Powell made his way through the crowd to join them. With him was the older girl he'd been with at Crandles's mansion. Over the noise of the celebrants, she told the MicroKidz about the dark side of the campaign.

"We were brought in from out of town, ten of us, and paid to disrupt things," the girl explained. "Hassle people at home, put up weird signs of the mayor, say that we worked for her and then insult the voters. It was mean."

"Dirty tricks," Thor stated.

"We only did it for the money, but when we found out the checks Ted Smyth gave us were worthless, it was game over," she sighed. "I didn't feel right about it then, and now I think it was just a stupid lesson for us."

She wandered off into the crowd.

"Not my type," said Kevin, "but I wanted you both to hear the dirt from her."

They were all relieved the competition was over. Politics brought out some peculiar qualities in people, not all of them honorable. The experience of dealing with their own beliefs in a public manner had been quite a lesson for the youngsters. They had seen democracy in action. They had participated in the electoral process. The MicroKidz had gained insights that would benefit them when they became old enough to vote themselves.

"But can we trust nationwide electronic voting?" wondered Pam.

"As much as the old ballot-by-pencil method," replied Thor. "There can be problems with that too. Every system has drawbacks."

"So what's the benefit? Is it just faster?"

"The major problem has always been getting the people out of their houses to vote. Most of the time, only 60 percent of eligible voters actually cast ballots. That means a government could run the country with only 31 percent of the people supporting it!"

"Now, excuses like 'The weather was too bad to go out,' or 'I didn't know where to vote,' or even 'I forgot' are gone," Kevin picked up. "But you know, it's a real shame that in our free country, where we have the right to vote, many people don't bother. Yet in other countries, people are killed for wanting to vote freely."

They'd had another lesson in democracy. People here had

the freedom to choose whether or not to become involved. Elsewhere there was no choice. And no freedom.

"Wow," breathed Pamela. "We sure do have a lot to be thankful for."

They were soon enveloped in the noise and excitement of the escalating celebration. Mayor Griffin made her way around, personally thanking her staff of volunteers. She was soon at the side of the trio.

"Pamela, you did a fantastic job. But I hope you have better luck convincing your brother the next time," the woman laughed. "And thanks again for the use of your robot, Thor. Any time Mr. Chips wants a job at City Hall, it's his!"

The youngsters wished her continuing success. She had her own wish for them.

"I'd like you to come to the town council inaugural," requested the mayor.

Once his computing equipment had been returned to his workshop, Thor Benson felt normal again. His father helped unload and restack the multitude of hardware.

"What's going to happen to that C.A.S.E.?" Thor asked while they were working. "Any chance we might get it?"

Edward Benson shook his head. "None at all. It was impounded by the government. They'll use it as an exhibit in the Crandles and Smyth trial. After that, it will probably be destroyed."

Thor felt that the device could be put to some beneficial use. However, he had no say in the matter, it was all out of his hands.

"You know, Dad, I'm glad you didn't hire me right away to work on the election."

His father was puzzled by the admission.

Thor explained. "Well, if I hadn't been doing that second-string work on the At-Home Shopping service, I wouldn't have come across all that background dealing."

"You're right about that. The early version of the C.A.S.E. that dipped into the system triggered the rest. Good thing you made that connection."

"That's what I'm getting paid for, right?"

Edward chuckled. "That reminds me. I'll have your pay, plus a bonus, transferred into your account."

"Just to be sure, Dad, could you pay me direct? Cash in an envelope? Like the old days when you were a kid."

"Thanks a lot!"

While they were laughing together, Pamela came to the door. Mr. Benson left them alone.

"You'd never notice anything changed in here," she said, glancing around the workshop.

"That was a great party last night," said Thor. "And Gwen Griffin is a real live wire."

"That's what she said about you. For the rest, wait until tomorrow," Pam hinted. "I guess you heard about that data dump in the Crandles headquarters. The sabotage that happened at the same time our system went down? It was all a setup. They didn't want anyone to get suspicious."

Thor saw that Pam was getting restless. She had forgotten how to relax.

"What about a trip to the Big Byte?" he prodded.

No, she'd already eaten.

"Well, maybe a night show at the Laserium?"

No, she'd seen that program twice before.

"Okay, let's go swimming!"

"Sure, but where?" There was no pool in the neighbourhood.

"Not a pool, Pam. Our hot tub!"

Bingo!

". . . and I'm sure the rest of the citizens of Stanton join me in thanking you, Thor Benson, for your achievements in ensuring fair, democratic elections within our area!"

As applause swept through the crowd in front of the podium, Mayor Gwen Griffin handed the youngster a gold plaque. On it was a platinum replica of the key to City Hall, mounted on a silver background. It glistened under the noonday sun, reflecting the fountains in front of City Hall.

The mayor wore her Chain of Office, having just been sworn in for a second term. Standing behind Thor were his parents, and Kevin and Pamela. The time had come for him to speak.

He couldn't move! Stage fright was Thor's weakness; he could not stand up and talk in front of people. This time he was saved from that embarrassment because, strangely, the public address system quit just as he was called on.

Instead, he asked Pam and Kevin to stand beside him while he held the plaque and posed for the cameras. As Kevin moved closer to Thor, he slipped a remote-control panel into his pocket. He had used the device to switch off the microphone, thus sparing Thor from having to make a speech!

One hundred miles above Stanton, in an orbiting satellite, trouble was about to erupt. It would require endurance, insight into space technology, and solid detective work on the part of the MicroKidz to deal with their next adventure mystery, *SATELLITE SKYJACK*.